Mission to
Metlakatla

Mission to
Metlakatla

Elaine Wentworth

HOUGHTON MIFFLIN COMPANY BOSTON

1 9 6 8

To Janet

ACKNOWLEDGMENTS

For their help and encouragement the author expresses her appreciation to her husband, Murray Wentworth; to her mother, Ingeborg Anderson, who typed and proofread the manuscript; and to Robert and Lucille Coleman, formerly of Alaska, who initiated the research. The author also gratefully acknowledges the office of the Commissioner of Indian Affairs, Robert L. Bennett, Washington, D.C., for information; Mr. J. W. D. Symons, Director, Maritime Museum of British Columbia, Victoria, B.C., for information about Captain Prevost and the H.M.S. *Satellite;* and the American Museum of Natural History, New York, for permission to sketch and take photographs in the Northwest Coast Indians Department.

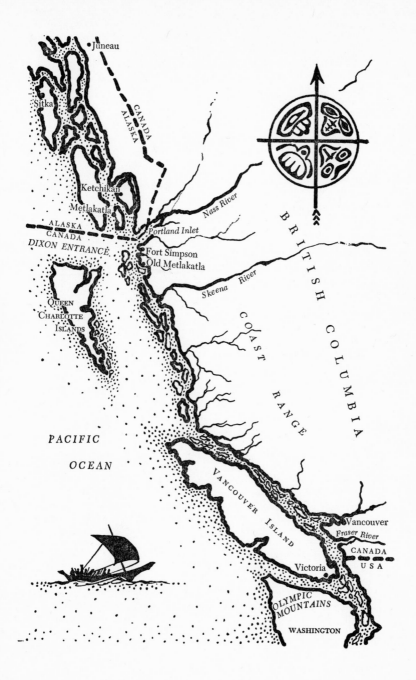

Mission to
Metlakatla

1

On a stormy night in December, 1853, in the town of Beverley, in Yorkshire, England, the chapel lights at Saint John's Church shone through the rain streaked windows and glittered invitingly out into the dark street. But few people had ventured out to attend the quarterly missionary meeting to be held that night.

Shaking his head sadly at the scanty audience, the Reverend Carr, vicar of the church, suggested that the visiting speaker might prefer to postpone his talk until another time. But the missionary insisted that those few who had braved the wind and rain were entitled to hear his message. Among the small congregation that night was William Duncan, then twenty-one years old. The rain and wind had soaked his sandy colored hair and drenched his clothes, but he seemed not to mind. With rapt attention he listened to the speaker tell of the desperate need for dedicated, energetic young men to serve in the foreign mission field.

It was still raining as he walked home after the meeting, but now the wet wind in his face only intensified

his feeling of excitement. Sleepless throughout the night, he pondered the question which persistently ran through his mind: "I was the only young man there . . . why shouldn't *I* become a missionary?" Before he finally fell asleep at dawn, he prayerfully decided he would accept the challenge.

Long accustomed to expect original ideas from young William, his family and friends were nevertheless amazed at his decision to become a foreign missionary. They urged him to consider cautiously all its aspects before deciding. But once William's mind was made up, no one could change it. He had always been like that, and they knew full well that opposition would only strengthen his determination.

His life so far seemed ordinary enough. He was born in 1832. At that time the American and Canadian West was still an unorganized frontier of hostile Indians. Explorers and fur trappers had broken trail through the wilderness, but few wagon trains had as yet raised their dust through Oregon Territory, whose exact boundary lines were still being disputed between England and America. England had no such wilderness in her homeland, but young English boys dreamed of the land of Indians just as young boys in America did.

In his childhood play eight-year-old William fearlessly encountered both Indians and devils. When he found an unaccounted-for penny in his pocket one day, he presumed it must be the work of the devil, for he had heard the grown-ups speak of the devil trying to buy' people. "The devil shall not buy *me*," shouted William, flinging the penny as far across the field as he could. All through his life William was just as quick to fling away any compromise with his beliefs.

Music was always a part of his life. As a young choirboy his soprano voice was so outstanding that people traveled long distances to hear him sing the solo parts at the Beverley Minster, the city's cathedral. Later, when his voice changed, he learned to play the accordion, the flute, and the piccolo.

At fifteen, William's school days well behind him, he became employed by a large leather tannery and wholesale dealer in hides, to copy letters and write out invoices in longhand. But the nimble-minded William quickly learned bookkeeping and was soon installed as the firm's accountant. Before his eighteenth birthday he was promoted again, this time to sales manager of the company.

3

Right from the start, William made up his mind to take his religious beliefs with him into business. His fair-minded policies suited the trend of the times, for England's lead in financial and industrial development was built more solidly on integrity than on shrewd speculations. Although his scrupulous approach was sometimes unique, it was apparent that it was also highly profitable, and the firm's executives soon found themselves letting young William run things his own way. This arrangement suited him well; beyond obeying God, Queen Victoria and the Church of England, he really did not care much for humbly following orders.

As William entered his twenties his eager mind reached out beyond business affairs for all the exciting news about new opportunities to serve in all the far-flung corners of the world — India, Africa, Australia, China, Canada. There seemed to be no place on the face of the earth where the British were not steadily gaining in influence. It was enough to make anyone restless, and it was in this new frame of mind that William returned to Beverley that rainy night to attend the missionary meeting at Saint John's Church.

When he informed his employers that he planned to become a foreign missionary, they were aghast and begged him to reconsider. They couldn't imagine why a young man of such ability would choose to give up a promising business career for one that held out no possibility whatever for financial gain. The owner of another larger firm, hearing that Duncan had given his notice, offered him the promise of a splendid partnership if he would come to work for him. But William's mind was made up. He gave his company six months' notice, and then entered Highbury College in London for three years' training to become a lay missionary for the Church of England.

In his study of the Bible at Highbury, William found a quotation by the Apostle Paul he particularly liked, and in his beautiful penmanship he copied it into his notebook, little knowing how deeply inscribed in his heart these words were to become: "This one thing I do, forgetting those things which are behind, and reaching forth unto those things which are before, I press towards the mark."

2

O N THE OTHER SIDE of the world, in the same year that William Duncan decided to become a foreign missionary, a British warship was steaming through the North Pacific. The *HMS Virago* zigzagged toward Alaska, through a winding maze of ocean channels, bounded on both sides by steep mountain slopes which rose abruptly from the sea. To the right rose the lofty icy chain of the coastal range, and to the left, in overlapping succession, the hundreds of forested islands which enclosed the Inside Passage.

The warship's duty in policing this intricate web of land and water was to protect the isolated English trading posts against Indian attacks. But just south of the Russian-Alaskan boundary line, the *Virago* developed engine trouble. Using the auxiliary sails, Captain Prevost immediately headed twelve miles southeast to Fort Simpson to make repairs.

This northernmost trading post of the Hudson's Bay Company was completely isolated from civilization. Rising out of the fog, its high walls and turrets reminded Captain Prevost of medieval castles in Europe. Under heavy guard from his warship he was rowed ashore and escorted up the beach to the fort, and as he passed by groups of painted Indians, the captain caught fleeting glimpses of their barbaric appearance. The sentinel on duty opened the ironbound double gate just wide enough to whisk the men inside.

The captain's keen eyes quickly took in the many marks in the walls of bullets fired by Indians who had attacked the fort. He observed that the high walls were built from the trunks of trees over three feet in diameter, driven into the ground and solidly riveted together. All around the inside walls, a gallery ena-

bled an armed guard to march back and forth, night and day, keeping watch on the surrounding area. The towers at each corner of the fort were mounted with cannon and manned by riflemen. It was obvious that Fort Simpson was in hostile territory.

Near the fort lived nine fierce Tsimshian Indian tribes, who were feared along the entire coastline by white men and Indians alike for their bloodthirsty savagery.

While his ship was being repaired Captain Prevost had time to study these savage Indians from an unobtrusive corner of the great storeroom. The clever Tsimshians were the established middlemen in the rich fur trade. In return for their candlefish they bartered land furs from the Interior Indians, never allowing them to deal directly with the Hudson's Bay Company. This privilege they reserved for themselves. Thus the wealthy coastal Tsimshians were able to bring to Fort Simpson the beaver, marten and mink skins of the Interior country, plus the hair seal, porpoise, sea lion and sea otter pelts so easily hunted in the ocean waters surrounding them.

When the Tsimshians approached to trade these furs, the guard cautiously allowed only two or three Indians at a time to enter the fort. They were admitted only through a narrow passageway which led to the great storeroom window where they could pass in their furs in exchange for store-goods, but care was taken not to display too exciting an array of supplies at any one time.

Since Captain Prevost could not safely leave the fort, he often took exercise by walking along the gallery. From there he could observe the Indians below. Their split-cedar houses lined the waterfront on both sides of the fort; their huge canoes beached in front of the houses on the narrow strip of rough sand. Many activities took place on this beach, for here the industrious Tsimshians prepared furs, steamed food, repaired canoes and carved and painted wooden utensils. At night the weird howling and the beating of the medicine drums filled the air with a chilling suspicion of the fiendish ceremonies being carried on in the dim firelight.

The captain, however, was filled with sympathy for these wild, superstitious children of the forest. It was easy to see that the white men had greedily taken advantage of these Indians for many years.

Seventy-five years before, in 1778, the seamen with Captain Cook had first traded a few pieces of iron with the Indians for sea-otter skins. When the expedition reached China, they discovered that the lustrous brown pelts were highly prized by the Chinese who were willing to pay fabulous prices for them. This news soon reached England, and it was not long before ships were outfitted for the voyage to the new land of treasure. For a few barrels of iron blades, roughly made knives, cheap glass beads and rum, they filled their holds with sea otter pelts worth a king's ransom in China.

Before long the Yankee skippers began to compete

in this profitable trade, too. Sailing their clipper ships from Boston to the Northwest Coast, they traded for furs which they sold in China for cargoes of tea, spices and silk. These in turn they sold back in Boston, eventually dominating a fantastically wealthy three-cornered trade.

Most of the seagoing traders did not expect to return, as the captain's share from a successful voyage netted him enough to retire on. Consequently, they had no interest in cultivating the goodwill of the natives. They did not hesitate to cheat or rob them when they could obtain furs no other way. Nor were they concerned that they were stripping the coast of the lovely sea otter. Eventually this precious animal was reduced to a small fraction of its original abundance, both in British Columbia and in Russian Alaska.

As the sea otter diminished, the sea traders began to

concentrate on land furs. But now they began to have competition from the American overland traders as more and more of them pushed west through Oregon Territory to the Pacific Northwest Coast. To cut off the flow of furs to both the American seagoing and land traders, the British Hudson's Bay Company built a chain of fortified trading posts, eventually penetrating deep into the northern wilderness. The most isolated post was Fort Simpson only twelve miles southeast of the Russian Alaska boundary line.

All these years that the white men had piled up fortunes in furs they showered over the Indians only disastrous fragments of civilization. The Indians had no resistance to the white men's diseases, and soon tuberculosis and smallpox had penetrated to the farthest villages. Nor had the Indians ever been exposed to intoxicating liquor, and the "hooch" they soon learned to distill for themselves was the worst of all — a deadly poison to their once vigorous health.

Captain Prevost, besides being a valiant naval officer, was also a concerned Christian gentleman, and he angrily realized that no effort was being made to counteract the Indians' tragic moral and physical decline. He was keenly aware that a missionary could do more than guns to transform the savage natives into happy peaceful human beings.

Captain Prevost said little about it, but the Tsimshian Indians continued to haunt him long after his departure from Fort Simpson. His desire to enlighten them grew rather than faded with the passing months.

3

THREE YEARS passed before Captain Prevost's Pacific Northwest duty ended and he was back in London. Once there he wasted no time telling his story about the Indians and his hopes for helping them. Although officials of the Church of England Missionary Society were enthusiastic, they declared there were no funds available to open a new foreign mission. They suggested that the captain write an article for their magazine, appealing to the public for funds. He gladly accepted and his eloquent plea met with quick response. They soon had $2,500 for the proposed mission.

The Missionary Society officials now had to find the right man to send to this new and dangerous mission field. Again and again they scanned their list of available candidates without coming to any decision.

Months went by and still they had not decided. Then Captain Prevost announced that he had been reappointed to his old station on the North Pacific Coast and would be sailing in a fortnight. This time he was to command a brand new warship, the *HMS Satellite*. What was even more important news, he had the Admiralty's permission to take along a missionary as far as Esquimalt on Vancouver Island.

Once again the Society met to go over their list. For the first time someone mentioned the name of William Duncan — somewhat hesitantly — for he was not experienced; indeed, he had not yet completed his three years of training. They all agreed he was one of the most promising students to graduate in the following spring. In fact he was already being considered for a future teaching assignment in India. William Duncan! The more they thought about it, the more certain they were that he had the qualities of strength and endurance they were seeking. Perhaps he really could be the right man — but would he go?

William's bright blue eyes sparkled when the suggestion was made to him. "I will go wherever I am sent," was the instant reply.

The next two days were a whirlwind of activity for William Duncan. By Friday he had organized and filed away his unfinished studies, packed his belongings including his accordion, and tied up all the loose ends of a young lifetime. He then headed for an outfitter's store and ordered an amazing variety of supplies including a shovel, saw, axe, rake and hoe, besides tools for carpentering and blacksmithing. When everything was ready to go, William counted twenty-eight pieces of bulky luggage.

He spent the weekend in Beverley saying farewell to his mother and friends. On Monday he took the express train to London to receive his final instructions, and the next morning William Duncan went aboard the *HMS Satellite*.

4

O<small>N</small> J<small>UNE</small> 13, 1857 after six long months at sea, the *Satellite* dropped anchor in Esquimalt Harbor. Duncan was rowed ashore in the captain's gig, but there was no one to welcome him as he first set foot on Vancouver Island, for not a soul was expecting him. Leaving his bulky luggage with the British Navy at Esquimalt, he set out alone for Fort Victoria, about three miles away.

Every few steps, however, he felt compelled to stop and gaze up in amazement at the great trees. Large dogwood bushes appeared as miniature plants beneath the giant fir trees that towered two hundred and fifty feet high.

Victoria then was only a tiny hamlet of about two hundred people living in cottages clustered around the fort. Beyond were the villages of the Nootka Indians. Wild roses bloomed in profusion along the woodland path that Duncan followed, and English honeysuckle and spirea had found a congenial home in the mild, foggy climate. Duncan thought he had never — not in all of England — breathed in anything like it; a shower had just ended and the air was filled to overflowing with a wet and dewy fragrance. The grain and vegetable gardens were as radiant as the fruit and flowers, and all this lush vegetation was growing out of fresh glacial soil. In the orchards peaches and apples fell upon glacier-polished rocks.

The fort, a group of log buildings surrounded by high picket palisades, was the center of all activity in the little village, for here was located the headquarters of the Hudson's Bay Company great Northwest Territory. Duncan was received at the fort by Sir James Douglas, head of the trading post and Governor of the Crown Colony of Vancouver Island as well. Sir Douglas, who at six feet six inches towered over the five foot six inch Duncan, was as erect and striking in appearance as the great trees. Behind his long face, large features and high forehead was a mind of penetrating insight.

Permission was required to travel farther north, and the fort was the official place to ask for it. But the governor had bad news for Duncan. He would not allow him to complete the last six hundred miles of his journey north in the company's steamer. He insisted that the Missionary Society had done a great wrong in sending a missionary to Northwest Territory without first consulting the company's officers.

"If I should allow you to go to Fort Simpson," said the governor, "it would be just the same as to send you to your certain death. This company cannot undertake to be responsible for your safety, and does not want to become a party to your murder." Instead the governor suggested, "Why not remain here? We have thousands of Indians in Victoria, not quite so savage, but who still need a missionary."

This was no solution to the dismayed Duncan. "The trouble is, Sir Douglas, that I am sent to Fort Simpson, and there I must go. If I cannot go there, I must return to England."

"But, young man, I know the situation up there, and you will not last three months among those savage and bloodthirsty Indians."

"Please, sir, just give me permission to go and stay in the fort until I can learn their language. I give you my word I will not leave the fort until I can speak to the Indians in their own tongue. Then I will go out and shift for myself, and the company need have no responsibility for my safety." But the governor wouldn't hear of it.

Duncan was bitterly disappointed. It would take a long time before word could return from London with new orders, and he could not contact Captain Prevost who had already sailed to the nearby San Juan Islands to help settle the boundary dispute between England and the United States. Nor could he contemplate stowing away, as the Hudson's Bay Company steamer which went north only twice a year, once in spring and again in fall, had already departed for the Northland. There was nothing he could do but endure his enforced stay in Victoria. He was invited to live with the

Reverend Cridge and his wife who had come from England several years before. At first a chaplain to the fort, the Reverend Cridge had since become pastor of a small church in the village. Duncan tried to make the best of his situation by helping him in any way he could. Although Duncan was not a clergyman, he conducted services on Sunday afternoons in a small settlement outside Victoria and led the young ladies' choir. He was well liked and made many friends. With the assistance of an Indian he began to learn Chinook, a simplified trading jargon common to both white men and Indians along the coast.

Still these were difficult days for Duncan. Geared for action, he did not find it easy to wait. He was also troubled by his own disgruntled feelings. The governor's suggestion that he might work among the Indians in Victoria was certainly sensible— perhaps he really could do more by staying right there. "After all, is not a missionary supposed to do God's work wherever he finds it?" thought Duncan. To satisfy his own adventuresome spirit was not supposed to be his purpose.

With the approach of autumn the Hudson's Bay Company steamer, the *Otter,* once more was loaded with supplies for the trip north. Again Duncan asked the governor's permission to go along and the governor, knowing him well now and admiring his determination to fulfill his dangerous assignment, this time yielded.

"Well, young man, if you are to be killed and eaten, I suppose you are the one most vitally concerned after all, and we shall just have to let you go; but promise me one thing — that you will never allow any Indians to enter the fort for a meeting."

Duncan bid farewell to Sir Douglas and made the rounds of the village saying good-bye to his many new friends. It was his last look at Victoria as an isolated island hamlet. Only a year later, when gold was discovered up the Fraser River, Victoria's character changed overnight. Men by the thousands rushed there to obtain permission to travel up the Fraser and to outfit themselves for the trip to the goldfields. Others came by the thousands to supply their wants. Even the established British settlers who had been leisurely reaping a slow but steady profit succumbed to the gold fever.

On September 25 the *Otter* steamed out of Esquimalt Harbor, headed north into the Gulf of Georgia, and began the five-day journey up the Inside Passage toward Alaska. Duncan took up his favorite spot on the forward deck of the *Otter*. To his amazement the steamer soon appeared to be running straight ashore. Suddenly, just as the prow almost touched the rocks, a narrow inlet opened to the right, the helm was swung hard to starboard, and the *Otter* slipped in between mountain walls rising from the sea. After a short distance the *Otter* made just as hard a swing to port and entered another shining passageway. Each winding turn was so different from the last that Duncan could hardly bear to leave the deck to eat or sleep.

He inhaled the damp fragrance from the trees lining

the shores — great stands of Douglas spruce, cedar and hemlock. In the narrowest channels the steamer was often so near the shore he could distinctly see the cones clustered on the tops of the trees and the ferns and bushes nestled at their feet. Glossy black ravens cawed from the lonely heights of the trees, their hoarse cries mingling with the noisy sea gulls following the *Otter*. Higher still, a snow-filled crag started a waterfall on its way, cascading and zigzagging down the mountainside until it finally broke the still surface of the channel. Duncan felt an instinctive response to some mysterious, primeval quality in all this wild, newborn scenery. He knew he would always love this solitary Northland.

Viewing this magnificent country in mellow sunshine, he thought it incredible that the hair-raising tales heard in Victoria could really be true: that bears and moose were not the wildest creatures roaming the dense forests. But the cheerful atmosphere was soon dispelled when the *Otter* plunged into a white wall of fog. The sun paled to a silver disk and then disappeared altogether, while the white wake of foam behind the steamer trailed off into mists. Now there was nothing definite left in sight except the squawking, mewing gulls dipping over the *Otter*. For the remainder of the journey the forecastlehead was barely visible from the door of the main cabin. The foghorn sounded its lonely blast day long and night long. Except for the ghostly shapes of passing headlands and islands, only the quickly returning echo of the foghorn indicated that land was definitely nearby. As they neared their destination a few patchy openings in the fog revealed small clearings in the forest, marked by tall and solemn totem poles.

Finally, after these long foggy days and nights, the *Otter*'s whistle announced their arrival at Fort Simpson, already in the darkness of a northern autumn afternoon. The repeated blast of the whistle created a stir of excitement in the fort and in the houses of the Indians along the shore. In the glare of their firebrands Duncan could see them running back and forth on the beach. As he was escorted to the fort by a heavy guard, Duncan noticed a group of Tsimshians following suspiciously behind, the dim red glow of firelight highlighting their tangled hair and glaring eyes. No sign of their capacity to become civilized men showed in their savage faces that night.

5

DUNCAN had barely settled into his small room at the fort when the excitement he sensed upon arrival increased in tempo both inside and outside the garrison. About twenty men were employed there while the nine tribes of Tsimshians totaled almost three thousand; and it appeared as though all nine tribes were planning to assemble on the beach below. As the crowd grew larger, guard duties were doubled and no one had time to bother with the new arrival. They were all busy keeping a sharp watch in every direction.

"What is going on? What are they planning to do?" Duncan asked the men on gallery lookout duty.

"It looks as if Chief Neyastodah is planning a potlatch," answered a guard. "He has probably made new claims that will increase his prestige among the other chiefs. These savages are terribly proud and vain. To show off his new wealth he will give away everything he owns — all his treasures — and those of his tribe, too. The greater the display, and the more gifts given away, the greater the glory for him and all his people."

For weeks the chief's own tribe had been presenting him with all they owned — canoes, guns, blankets, furs — everything fit to give away. The day before the great potlatch took place the gifts were brought down to the shore and publicly displayed. Hundreds of yards of calico were unrolled and paraded along the beach. Beautifully carved and painted wooden masks and feast dishes were lined up for all to admire. Single file, bearers paraded up and down with Chilkat blankets, copper shields and furs held high aloft on long poles. After all the gifts were thus proudly displayed, they were carried in triumph to the house of Chief Neya-stodah. All the gifts were his now. His people had given up their valuable possessions for the sake of the social standing of their tribe, which was certain to benefit from the increased honor of their chief.

On the great day of the potlatch the crowd gathered to wait for the chiefs of the other eight tribes to arrive. A strong wind whipped the surface of the gray water into ragged whitecaps. In the open sea beyond the harbor long breaking waves began to dash against the rocks.

"Shimauget," "Shimauget," yelled the Indians as the first canoe was sighted rounding a headland. Then into the harbor swept fleets of enormous and magnificent canoes, their high projecting bows spraying foam in all directions. Hollowed out of one giant log, each canoe was over fifty feet long and paddled by many slaves. As they approached the shore Duncan could see how strangely yet beautifully carved and deco-

rated they were. Swiftly and expertly, with a great swishing and scraping on the rough sand, the canoes were run up on the beach beyond the high tide line.

The chiefs stood regally near the stern decked out in their full ceremonial regalia. Out of the most elaborately decorated canoe stepped Chief Legaic, highest ranking chief of all nine tribes. Befitting his status he wore a carved wood ceremonial headdress representing the raven, his totemic emblem. The details of the carved design were accented with red, black and blue-green paint and inlaid with abalone shell. The lofty headpiece was surmounted with sea lion bristles and draped with ermine skins which fell in a mantle across the chief's shoulders and down his back. His Chilkat blanket of mountain goat's wool was woven with stylized designs representing the killer whale in black, yellow and green, with the natural white of the wool left in many sections of the design. Feathers, shells, polished bones and embroidered porcupine quills adorned his costume, and as he sedately walked ashore, the fringe on his dancing apron jingled with puffin beaks.

Now that Chief Legaic had arrived the guests paraded into the house of their host to dance, feast and receive their gifts. Inside the great house the chiefs were seated according to their rank, for the Tsimshians observed the strictest rules of rank and class. Chief Neyastodah consulted his bundle of memo-sticks continuously. A herald loudly announced each gift and with great pomp delivered it to the proper guest. As each gift was accepted, Chief Neyastodah became poorer and poorer, but this fact bothered him not at all, for he had experienced the glory of a potlatch that would be spoken of for many moons. He also knew he was sure to get everything back with interest at the next potlatch given by one of his guests, and consequently, he kept accurate account of every item given away. It was the Tsimshian way of banking and insurance.

Of course the people at the fort couldn't see the potlatch taking place, but when the feasting and dancing began they could hear it without any straining. The furious hammering and screeching kept up for hours as dancers wearing imaginative costumes and movable masks enacted the ancient legends.

26

"Listen to that racket!" exclaimed one of the officers. "Just wait, before this murderous game of swap is over someone is bound to be killed. The least little injury to someone's vanity and savage revenge can be expected. I've never seen a potlatch yet that didn't end in a murder."

"That's right," spoke another officer. "The Devil Dancers will whip them all into hysterics; the Medicine Men will rattle them into fiendish rites; the Dog Eaters Club and the Cannibal Club will feel compelled to perform their orgies, and the whole bloody affair will wind up in a howling frenzy."

Just as they predicted, the potlatch whirled toward its frenzied climax. After a long, bloodcurdling scream

it became apparent that a slave had been murdered — probably to avenge an insult to a guest chief — and the poor body dragged out onto the dark beach. All the guests then followed to see what would happen next. Two medicine men appeared and began to dance and jerk their way through the crowd, their shriveled old bodies encased in wolfskins with the heads forming helmets. Jangling with charms — dried skunkskins, distended fishbladders, eagle claws, engraved bones and teeth — they howled and gestured until the Cannibal Club members encircled the murdered body. Then with more howlings the members proceeded to tear the body apart with their teeth and eat it. In the dark and confusion it was difficult to see any details, and that night Duncan believed that they really did devour their victim to the accompaniment of the medicine drums. But the Cannibal Club even managed to fool the uninitiated among their own people. They acted as if they chewed up the morsels of human flesh, and they pretended to swallow it, but at the crucial moment they spat it out and cleverly managed to substitute animal meat instead.

Spattered with blood the hysterical "cannibals" danced and leaped by the firelight, filling even their own people with terror, and reminding Duncan of ravenous wolves in their ferocity. At last, with his own eyes he had witnessed the bloodthirsty savagery of which Governor Douglas had so persistently warned him.

Now he could see how frail and insufficient was his

youthful optimism; he could see that without God's guidance every step of the way, he would indeed be killed and eaten before he could even begin his mission among them. So steeped in tribal superstitions were the Tsimshians, and so filled with savage pride and revenge, Duncan knew it would take more than preaching to unlock the door to their hearts. It would also take a long, long time — perhaps a lifetime would be too short — but standing there on the gallery he earnestly prayed that God would give him the strength and wisdom he needed. Even as he prayed, however, his practical mind began to formulate a plan, and it wasn't long before he knew precisely just how he would begin.

6

Duncan's first step was to learn the Tsimshian language. So far no white man had mastered it. Indian and white traders used a combination of simple words and signs called Chinook jargon, but this was incomplete for teaching purposes. Literal translations into Chinook were often misleading and ridiculous; for instance, "children of the forest" translated into Chinook merely signified "little men among many sticks," and for this dubious greeting one could be murdered. Duncan knew it would be folly to address them until certain he could be clearly understood.

It was a complicated language, rich in picturesque, expressive figures of speech and soft flowing sounds, for despite their barbarity, the Tsimshians were highly intelligent — far superior to the nomadic Indians of the Plains. The Northwest Coast Indians had no need to be nomads; theirs was a settled way of life. Since the sea and forest so easily yielded them an amazing wealth of fish, game and timber, they found plenty of leisure time to develop their talents and abilities. After the summer fishing season was over, after all the salmon, candlefish and wild berries were dried and preserved for winter, they had time to develop a complex culture in which men, animals, fact and fancy were all interwoven. These social and religious concepts were symbolically expressed through their elaborate dancing ceremonies, through their ancient legends, and most dramatically of all, through their stylized, intricate works of art.

To reach this inner life of the Tsimshians, Duncan knew he must gain a complete understanding of the tongue in which they formulated their thoughts. Somehow, he would have to learn it — without a dictionary, without a grammar, without an alphabet, and in as short a time as possible; for he had promised the governor he would not leave the fort until he could speak to them in their own language. Somewhere he would have to find a teacher; and since no white man could help him, he would have to find an Indian language teacher.

The captain of the fort helped him choose a young Ligaket from Chief Legaic's tribe who often came to trade his furs for iron blades and carving tools. "Ligaket" meant an Indian of aristocratic birth who had inherited the right to become a counselor to a chief. This young Ligaket, named Clah, was about twenty-three years old, Duncan's age, and had impressed everyone at the fort with his quick mind and calm manner. He occasionally acted as an interpreter at the fort since he knew the Chinook jargon. Free to spend

most of his time as he chose, Clah was happiest when occupied with carving and painting house poles, canoes, feast dishes, and all the equipment and utensils the wealthy Tsimshians desired decorated.

After Clah had agreed to come every day, Duncan made a list of fifteen hundred of the most common and useful words in the English language. His first task was to learn these words in Tsimshian, and to write them down phonetically, as they were pronounced by Clah. Clah knew no English, and Duncan no Tsimshian, but they both knew the Chinook jargon, and when that failed, they used signs, gestures and objects. It was not so difficult while the object of the word was at hand and could be pointed out, as a house, man, nose, eye, chair or table, but when it came to words beyond what was visible, the task required rare ingenuity.

When Duncan wanted to learn the Tsimshian expression for "try," he took a slate, wrote "Clah" in big letters and showed him the writing. Then rubbing out what he had written, he handed the pencil to Clah and pointed to the slate. Clah, who could not write, shook his head.

"Try, try!" Duncan urged with eager gestures. But Clah only shook his head again. Then he took Clah's hand and guided it so that he was able to write the word "Clah." Then pronouncing it, and pointing to the word, and then to the blank space below, he handed Clah the pencil. Again he repeated, "Try! try!"

A light of understanding now came into Clah's black eyes. As he took hold of the pencil he exclaimed, "Tumpaldo! tumpaldo!" Duncan ran over to the fireplace, grabbed hold of a heavy log, and pretended to attempt to lift it. Unable to do so, he cried, "Tumpaldo! tumpaldo!" "Ah, ah!" nodded Clah, which in Tsimshian meant "Yes, yes."

Sometimes hours went by before Duncan could find the Tsimshian expression for one English word. But while Duncan was slowly building his Tsimshian vocabulary, something he had not counted on was happening. Clah was learning English! As Clah said years later, "Yes, Mr. Duncan teach me English, and me teach him Tsimshian."

This mutual teaching was a great help to Duncan as he advanced from single words to sentences. Days, weeks, then two months went by as Duncan and Clah struggled together, each learning from the other. The drizzly rains of autumn gave way to the wet gales of winter and by January Duncan was able to write out the Tsimshian expressions for twelve hundred short sentences. C705789 CO. SCHOOLS

Meanwhile, as the relentless torrent poured down and the gales howled around the fort, something wonderful was happening; something Duncan had not foreseen. Clah was fast becoming his devoted friend. In their long hours together Clah felt, more than he could express, the powerful love and determination of his new friend. He became convinced that Duncan had truly come to bring good news to his people, and he eagerly told them so. Again and again he explained to his father and friends that the young white man had come, not to barter and trade, not to buy their women, not to peddle whiskey, but to bring them a message from the white man's God; and to teach them the knowledge of those things in which the white man was superior to the red man.

No white man having ever expressed concern for them before, the Indians found this difficult to comprehend, but their curiosity was aroused. Especially curious were the chiefs and wise men of the tribes who, Clah knew, were deeply troubled about the future of their people. He had listened as the chiefs sat around the central fire and talked of this haunting fear. They were aware that the increasing number of white men in their land was a threat to their ancient heritage.

Primitive though they were, they had their own strict codes of honor. Clah knew this. He had sat by the fire during the long winter nights while his uncles had instructed him in the accepted codes of behavior, and the responsibilities of his inherited rank. He had been taught to be brave and industrious. Laziness, in particular, was frowned upon for all, even those of the ruling class. With the other children he had eagerly listened to the lessons learned through the ancient legends. They had heard the way in which the raven had secured for them the sun, the moon and stars, and had listened to hundreds of other fascinating stories. In the huge dim house, lit only by the crackling fire with the smoke and sparks vanishing through the smoke hole into the night, the stories were vividly impressed upon their imaginative minds.

But the white man's influence was beginning to undermine the mystical power of the ancestral legends. As the Indians tried to copy the white man's ways, their own social patterns began to crumble with nothing of value gained to take their place. Even their health was in danger. The chiefs knew that the population was already decreasing at an alarming rate along the coast. Iron cutting blades and better carving tools were hardly worth the ravages produced by the white man's diseases. The chiefs were tragically aware that they had no power to halt this decline, and especially did they grieve for their children and grandchil-

dren. A few more moons, a few more years, and the following generations of Tsimshians might tread the dark forest with only a memory of their former way of life.

Frequently now, as the winter winds blew sodden rain clouds below the mountaintops, the Indians inquired of Clah when the white man would be able to speak to them. But Duncan was not yet ready. He was making a special study to frame his speech in that peculiar figurative language that appealed most directly to the Indians' understanding. Late into the night his lamp flickered as he wrote, revised, and rewrote.

His only diversion during these lonely months was to walk along the gallery of the fort. Whenever a letup in the gales of rain made it possible, Duncan hurried up the gallery stairs to watch the mist-shrouded islands come and go like mirages in the foggy sea. As soon as the rain stopped, the air became fresh and bracing with the scent of forest, sea and drying lumber. More than ever Duncan longed to leave the confinement of the fort — to walk along that briny, rocky beach and enter into the pathless woods.

7

To WALK ANYWHERE at all began to seem like a great adventure as long as it meant getting outside the fort. Clah was eager to take him on his first trip outside, and was certain he could safely guide his friend through the Indian village. Although not yet ready to speak to the Indians as a group, Duncan could easily make himself understood by Clah, and so in spite of the fort captain's warnings, they decided to venture forth together.

Clah first guided his friend to his own home where he knew Duncan would be warmly received in spite of all the warnings from the fort to the contrary. This was Duncan's first opportunity to enter a Tsimshian community house.

In front of it towered a sixty-foot-high cedar column, carved and painted with designs of animals representing the legends and symbols of Clah's clan. In order to fit all the designs onto the pole, the stylized animals and birds were distorted into interlocking positions with the figures above and below. The totem pole had been erected as a memorial to one of Clah's relatives.

Clah ran his hand expertly over the textured surface. It was the first totem pole he had personally designed and supervised, and he was pleased with the result. Although only a few years old, the carved wood had already weathered to a rich shade of pewter. The mineral colors — red, brown, yellow and bluish-green — derived from ocher and copper, and used to accent the details, had also weathered and blended harmoniously with the soft gray wood.

Built on a framework of heavy posts and beams, the house was almost square, about fifty-five feet wide and sixty-five feet long. Duncan could see from the outside that it was a large house; nevertheless, upon entering he was amazed at the expanse of the one huge room. The supporting columns, called house posts, were about three feet wide and fifteen feet high; these too were carved and painted with the totemic crests of the family, and with figures illustrating traditional family legends.

Around the sides of this cedar-planked room an elevated platform furnished storage and sleeping quarters for the various families who lived there. All sorts of paraphernalia — ceremonial dancing costumes and movable wooden masks, furs, blankets and carved feast dishes — were stored in decorated chests along this platform.

In the center of the room, on the lowest level, a large

fire pit was ablaze and hissing with damp logs, and directly above, an opening in the gabled roof allowed the smoke and sparks to escape.

Picking up a spruce root basket, Clah emptied some dried candlefish into the fire. Immediately the fire flared high, sending flickering light into the dim shadows of the platform. In the brightness Duncan could see that all the storage chests and boxes were also carved and painted with symbolic animal designs. Across the supporting beams dried fish were strung on strips of bark, making a sort of inner roof.

Inviting Duncan to sit near the fire, Clah spread out a cedar-bark mat and placed the feast dishes upon it. Small children hung back in the shadows of the room and eyed the visitor with great curiosity. They could see that Clah considered the young white man's visit a festive occasion, for only at such times did the young men of the household serve the meal.

Duncan was touched by his friend's obvious pleasure in making him feel welcome and honored. Since the everyday meal usually consisted of only two dishes, Duncan realized that this was a feast spread before him, and he tried to partake enthusiastically of every course.

The dried roasted salmon, clams, animal fats and meats, seaweed soups and berries were all appetizing dishes, if only the inevitable candlefish grease had not been generously poured over them all. Only the Soopalally seemed free from grease. This last and special treat was a frothy liquid made from dried soapberry cakes, mashed and crumbled into water, and then whipped into a foamy liquid of the consistency of thick soup. No feast was complete without a final serving of Soopalally which was flicked into the mouth from a flat spoon made especially for this purpose.

After several visits to this house, Clah took Duncan to visit others in the village. This gave him a chance to meet many Indians in a friendly, informal way and helped dispel their suspicious notion that he was some supernatural being.

Whenever he learned of anyone's being sick he ministered to him with simple advice interpreted by Clah, and occasionally gave medicine from his own supplies.

Gradually a few began to respond to his kindness to them.

By these visits to the houses of all classes of Tsimshians, Duncan gained an insight into their lives, familiarized himself with their customs, and even before having spoken to them formally, unlocked a special entrance into a few hearts.

Early in March the cold winds subsided and the first candlefish were sighted coming over the bar in Portland Inlet, and heading upstream into the Nass River, fifty-five miles to the Northeast. Soon millions of the greasy little candlefish would be hurrying over the shoals into the great river, and the Tsimshians intended to be right there at their ancient fishing grounds to catch them.

Duncan was temporarily forgotten as day and night they fished for their winter's supply of Oolakan (candlefish).

Not until the end of April, when the last drop of grease was extracted from the fish, did they catch their breath and have time to think again about the strange white man at the fort. Resting around the campfires, they once again wondered what Duncan planned to say to them. It was rumored all over the Nass River camp that Duncan really had a message from God. By the time they returned to Fort Simpson curiosity ran so high that Chief Neyastodah decided to pay Duncan a visit at the fort.

"I have heard that you have come here with the letter of God. Is that so? Have you the letter of God with you?" asked the chief.

"Yes, I have God's Letter," said Duncan.

"I want to see it."

Duncan placed his large Bible on the table, saying, "This is God's Book, God's Letter."

"Chief Neyastodah reverently, almost caressingly, laid his hand on the Bible.

"Is God's Letter for the Tsimshians?"

"Certainly. God sent this Book to all races; to your people as well as to mine."

Duncan wanted to be sure the chief understood that he had not brought a message from England, not from the Queen or from anyone else, but from the God who had created them both. When the chief understood that, he began to pause and think, and desired to know more about it.

"Does that Book give God's Heart to us?"

"It does."

"And are you going to tell the Indians that?"

"I am."

"Ahm! Ahm! Shimauget!" (It is good, it is good, chief.)

When Chief Neyastodah returned and told the other Indians about his visit, about the message in God's Book, they could hardly wait until Duncan was ready to bring it to them.

8

Duncan was just as eager to give his first message as the Tsimshians were curious to hear it. For eight lonely months he had struggled with their language and thoughtfully considered all aspects of their native culture, and as usual he had formed definite opinions. He had seen their most savage rites from a moonlit gallery and then saw another side to these complex people by day; his thoughts about them had clarified and strengthened. He realized that the Indians ridiculed the idea of ever accepting the white man's teaching. They had their own notions about God and the creation of the universe based on generations of legends and lore. Some of these concepts, however, embraced ideas which Duncan believed might make it possible for them to understand his message eventually.

Their religious beliefs were intertwined with mythology and were not easily defined; the supernatural world played an important part in the life of each Indian from childhood until death. They believed that animals had immortal spirits and supernatural powers which might be used to harm or benefit man; and that all men, animals, trees, plants and every growing thing were habitations for these spirits. Like all perceptive people they were keenly aware of their beautiful sea in the forest and longed to understand its mysteries. They too, asked the immortal questions about man and nature: "Who am I? Where is God? Who sends the wind? Who sends the salmon rushing upstream year after year?"

But beyond their belief in supernatural animals, the Tsimshians also believed in a Great Spirit above them all; a Heavenly Chief (Shimauget Lahaga) who was immortal and observed all that was going on among men. Clah had told Duncan the legend of the Stone and the Elderberry Bush which described the creation of man, and the legend about the Great Flood which described how the Tsimshians came to the Nass River Country.

That they had a concept of prayer, Duncan had observed for himself at the home of Clah. Before eating, the chief had taken a small piece of salmon and put it on the fire, saying, "For the Heavenly Chief, the first."

One thing he knew for certain — when he talked to the Indians he would bury all church creeds and doctrines and go simply in the name of God. He would not attack these people in their ancient customs; he would not ridicule them or speak against them wantonly. Believing they had all the qualities necessary to make civilized men of themselves, he would let God's word itself develop the Indians. With these convictions in his heart, and his sermon stuffed in his pocket, he was ready to begin.

Out of respect to their tribal customs he wished to address the people in their own homes and asked Clah to seek permission of the nine chiefs and to arrange a suitable time.

The great day was set for June 13, 1858, exactly one year after his arrival in the Northwest. It dawned clear and sunny. Clah appeared at the fort impressively decked out for the occasion in a Chilkat blanket, dancing apron and headdress. It had not occurred to Duncan that Clah would wear his ceremonial costume, and he could not help chuckling to himself at their rare contrast in appearance: Clah, a dazzling sight in his decorative robes, and Duncan, so plain and proper in his dark English clothes. But only in appearance were they worlds apart. Duncan sensed that Clah, too, in spite of his stately manner, was just as tense and excited as he was.

As they ventured forth together they noticed that not one canoe had left the beach that bright Sunday morning.

Their first stop was at the house of Chief Neyahshnawah where one hundred Indians were gathered to hear him. This was the first Indian assembly Duncan had ever faced. His heart was pounding and his throat felt dry. One word improperly used might produce an entirely wrong impression; one mispronounced might bring ridicule on the messenger and the message.

However, he did not yield to the temptation to read his sermon sentence by sentence to Clah, and let him interpret it to the waiting throng. He started by asking the Indians to close the entrance. This brought a mood of stillness over the audience which was heightened by Duncan's kneeling down for a few moments of silent prayer. He then gave them the first speech they had ever heard from a white man in their native language.

All through the speech the Tsimshians were silent and listened attentively. Duncan then said good-bye to this group and went to Chief Legaic's house where a sail was spread out for him to stand on. One hundred and fifty Indians were gathered there, advised by their chief to behave themselves.

He went to the other seven chiefs' houses, Clah es-

corting him, and in each repeated his address.

By four o'clock that afternoon, without stopping for lunch, he had preached in nine different houses, reaching about eight hundred or more Tsimshians.

Clah, who had closely observed the attitude of the Indians throughout the day, assured Duncan that judging from their faces, he thought they must have felt it to be "good." But that night alone in his room where he could reflect upon the day, Duncan knew the truth was that they were all superstitiously afraid of him. It was mostly with feelings of fear and contempt they approached him to hear God's Word, and when he prayed among them he prayed alone. None understood. None responded. Still he had begun, and hopefully he prayed that someday love would take the place of fear and light the place of darkness.

9

Duncan's next step was to start a school. Chief Legaic, not in the least inclined toward Duncan's religion, was nevertheless anxious that his people should not miss the material advantages of the white man's knowledge. Shrewdly recognizing the value of a school, he immediately offered the use of his own house.

Twenty-six children answered the morning roll call on the first day. Only fifteen Indians attended the afternoon class for adults, as it took more courage for the older people to attend the school. Then too, those outside of Legaic's tribal family felt uneasy in the house of the head chief. One chief informed Duncan, "You will have all the people to teach as soon as you have your own schoolhouse."

Duncan thought this over. Chief Legaic was soon planning to leave his house for the Skeena River fishing grounds, and with practically everyone going off to fish for salmon there would be hardly anyone left in the village to attend school until the salmon run was over. He decided to postpone the classes until the Indians had time to help him build the schoolhouse.

In past years Clah had always fished for salmon as they fought their way upstream to spawn and die. Everyone fished with all kinds of equipment — harpoons, nets, traps — for the season was short, and enough salmon had to be caught for a full winter's supply. But this season Clah remained at the Fort Simpson village to protect his friend.

Although Clah did not dare take his friend any great distance, he began to acquaint Duncan with the woods behind the village. One sunny July day he guided Duncan through the forest to a small salmon stream. There were no paths through the tangled underbrush, but Clah cleared the way for them, brushing aside the skunk cabbage, vines and thorny devil's club that thrived in the damp shade of the giant trees. The spongy layers of muskeg underfoot gave an extra spring to their bounding leaps over rotting stumps and logs. On the mossy trunk of a fallen spruce hundreds of seedling trees grew in crowded profusion, forming a fairylike forest in miniature with ferns and mushrooms adding to the elfin effect. A red squirrel, twirling a mushroom around as he nibbled away on its edges, scolded their intrusion into his private woodland. Its chittering was the only sound as they made their way deeper into the dark woods. Only slivers of sunlight penetrated the dense growth and sifted down through

dangling veils of moss hanging from the trees. Only the snapping twigs underfoot broke the deep silence until they heard the gushing of the rapids.

Reaching the stream Clah and Duncan crouched behind some rocks where they could watch for bears without being noticed. Presently a mother bear crunched out of the woods and made her way across the rapids on a fallen log, with two cubs trailing obediently behind her. After nudging the cubs to a safe spot by the water's edge, she waded into the foaming water to catch a salmon for her family. The salmon were leaping into the air all around her, and in a few minutes she had caught a fish in midair with a snap of her heavy jaw.

Another scuffling was heard in the woods and a larger bear lumbered into view. It was Old-Broken-Jaw. Plopping down in midstream he waited patiently, his broken jaw hanging ajar, until a luckless salmon leaped smack into his gaping mouth.

After the bears went back to the woods, Duncan stretched out on a rock to watch the salmon. Jumping from pool to pool they leaped high into the air above the rapids, their silvery bodies sparkling and shimmering in the sunlight. Not all these flashing leaps were successful; many salmon dashed themselves against the rocks and fell back into crevices and pools to thrash and die. Above them other salmon hurtled on, often bruised and bleeding from their relentless journey upstream.

Watching the spectacular sight of the annual salmon

run, Duncan could easily understand why the Tsimshians called the salmon "chiefs" and ceremoniously greeted the first fish of the season as welcome guests. The Indians believed "that the salmon were a race of supernatural beings who dwelt in a great house under the sea. There they went about in human form, feasting and dancing like people. When the time came for the 'run,' the salmon-people dressed themselves in garments of salmon flesh; that is, assumed the form of fish to sacrifice themselves. Once dead, the spirit of each fish returned to the house beneath the sea. If the bones returned to the water, the being resumed his humanlike form with no discomfort, and could repeat the trip next season. Since the salmon-people's migration upstream was considered to be voluntarily undertaken, it followed that it behooved human beings to take great pains not to offend their benefactors."

Consequently, in order to continue good relations with these important beings, the Tsimshians evolved many rituals and taboos referring to the salmon. They were never cooked in metal. Only special wooden kettles were used so as not to "shame" the salmon. To return all the salmon bones to the water was another procedure believed to be essential. "If some bones were thrown away on land, on resurrection the salmonperson might lack an arm or a leg, or some other part, and he and his tribe would become angry and refuse to run again in the stream in which they had been so unappreciatively treated."

When the tribes returned from salmon fishing they

still had no time to build the schoolhouse, for now they turned their complete attention to smoking, drying and preserving their winter's supply of food. In addition to salmon, the halibut, herring and clams were dried and stored. Soups were made from seaweed, and fruits and berries were gathered — crab apples, cherries, huckleberries, salalberries, soapberries and saskatoons — to be eaten fresh or dried for winter. For storing, the berries were cooked to a pulpy mass, poured into wooden containers lined with skunk cabbage leaves and then dried into cakes. Not until summer's end when all the activity subsided did the Indians again have the leisure time to help Duncan build his schoolhouse.

Early in the morning of the day set to begin building, Duncan hurried to the end of the beach where a large raft was anchored. The heavy logs had been previously cut and rafted over to a spot not far from the proposed building site. Only one old Indian waited on the raft. After a while two or three more appeared. Then two chiefs arrived, followed by several more Indians. Eventually a few more ambled over and sat down, Indian-style, as though only intending to look on. After an hour went by without anyone else joining them it seemed apparent that this was all the help he would have. Compared to their previous enthusiasm, Duncan was surprised and disappointed by this glum little gathering, but knowing it was of no use to push the Indians, he patiently waited a little longer.

About 7 A.M. one of the Indians on the raft sprang to

his feet and gave the whooping yell for starting. Duncan preceded them up the hill to the building site, while the small group, so inadequate for the huge task, began to carry the logs ashore. All of a sudden there was a great whooping yell from one of the Indians, followed by more whooping and yelling that came from all directions. Wheeling around, Duncan was amazed to see that the original number had grown in that instant to more than forty Indians!

They all moved at once and sprang to work with the most alarming enthusiasm and racket. The whole camp became excited, and the heavy blocks and beams began to move up the hill with incredible speed. The Indians declared they would not stop until the work was done, but by three o'clock Duncan insisted they all go home and rest till the next morning.

He was greatly relieved to see them quit for the day, for the constant whooping, groaning and bawling of the Indians, together with the great difficulty of the work kept him in constant fear of a mishap. Completely exhausted, Duncan fell into bed that night with their shouts still ringing in his ears.

Within a few days the framework was in position and the work of finishing the school and providing it with desks and benches went on with speed. Duncan had intended to buy bark for the roof, but the Indians, insisting that the white chief's teaching house ought to have a roof of boards, donated with a great deal of ceremony and show of good feeling, the boards for both floor and roof. Many who could not otherwise have contributed brought boards from their own houses.

On November 17, a triangle of metal was rung for a bell, and all Duncan's former pupils plus many new students rushed eagerly into the finished schoolhouse. In all, the attendance was one hundred and forty children and fifty adults, many more than he had ever expected to see there. There was a greater desire for instruction than he had ever realized. Also, a strong feeling prevailed that the white man possessed some grand secret about eternal things which they were intensely anxious to know, even if it involved the overthrow of their most cherished superstitions.

There was one group of men among the Tsimshians, however, to whom the school was extremely displeasing. The Shoo-wansh (medicine men) saw in Duncan's teachings the utter destruction of their witchcraft, for with education and enlightenment, the people would ultimately cease to believe in their empty sorceries; and the medicine men would tumble from their high positions as priests of the savage rites. They secretly determined to get rid of their enemy.

10

THE MEDICINE MAN (Shoo-wansh, meaning "the blower") was a very important person in the Tsimshian community. But he was not the most practical physician of the tribes. The use of herbs as potions and as applications for wounds was in the hands of wise old women. The medicine man was called in to heal an illness that could not be treated in this way. When there was no apparent explanation for an illness, the Indians suspected that the person had been bewitched. This type of ailment the medicine man could handle expertly.

He came with his rattle to drive out the evil spirits that had taken possession of the poor suffering victim. His badge of office was his shaggy tangle of hair which he never cut or combed. Donning one of his movable wooden masks he began his cure. He rattled and chanted and danced about with wild gestures; he blew into the patient's nose and mouth, pounded his body, and howled and shrieked until the harassed patient said he felt better. Then, blowing through an exquisitely carved bone tube, the medicine man retrieved the patient's soul, which he claimed to have caught leaving the body. The medicine men were extremely clever at performing magical tricks. Every prominent tribal family had its own special trick — a family secret — known only to the chief and his medicine man. Chief Legaic and his medicine man, Cushwat, had a special trick they performed together on special occasions — an impressive one for showing supernatural power. Cushwat killed his chief by cutting off his head. The body of Chief Legaic toppled over, the head rolled to the floor, and with the blood squirting out, jumped from one end of the room to the other. It was a most lively cut-off head.

The other Indians "died," which is their expression for amazement. But still greater was their astonishment when Cushwat twisted the head back onto the body, and, after fumbling around and smearing the cut place with grease, brought the chief back to life again — speaking, laughing and dancing around as if he had never "lost his head" at all.

It was not a difficult trick with the chief as an accomplice. A false head and mask were set above his own head which was concealed under his dancing blanket. By operating a set of strings, the false head, provided with bags of blood, was made to jump around the floor. When the false head was put back on again, it was actually hidden in the folds of the blanket while the chief's own head emerged and began to speak and laugh.

In the dim light of the central hearth, tricks such as these were extremely effective as the stage props were not easily seen. Many houses had tunnels and trapdoors so that actors could appear and disappear. Lines of hollow kelp stems were concealed under the floor and used as speaking tubes, causing performers' voices to come from unexpected places. Puppets and monsters flew across the room on strings. Many of the Indians were completely fooled by these sensational stage effects, and those who were not fooled enjoyed them anyway.

Much later, when Duncan began to ridicule the medicine men and their practices, his followers begged him to be careful not to put himself in their power. "When you cut your hair, be sure to burn it all up, so they will not get hold of any of it and bewitch you," they warned him. But Duncan, in order to show that he was not afraid, told them that the next time he cut his hair he would send a lock of it to each medicine man in camp so he could have some to work on.

In spite of their power and prestige the medicine men did not dare go against the wishes of the chiefs; and Chief Legaic, although personally indifferent to Duncan's teachings, nevertheless had offered his own home for the first schoolroom and was treating the white man with consideration. Since they dared not harm Duncan without Chief Legaic's permission, they waited until an opportune moment when they could persuade Legaic to turn against him, too. In December they had their chance.

Chief Legaic went to the captain of the fort to inform him that his young daughter had "gone to the moon" for her education. As a part of this ritual the medicine men were busy performing mysterious rites in Chief Legaic's house; and he was afraid the children, noisily passing by on their way to school, might be harmed by the medicine men if they interfered with the mysteries. He therefore wanted the captain to persuade Duncan to close the school for one month.

Duncan of course would not hear of it. "Not for a month, not even for a day will I close. Satan has reigned long enough here. It is high time his rule should be disturbed."

The captain wiped his head in exasperation while the second officer said, "I think you are making a grave mistake, sir, in not giving in to them. You do not know what you are doing. You ought to respect their superstitions. It is likely that bloodshed will come of this."

"Well, sir," replied Duncan, "if blood will be shed, it certainly will not be yours, anyhow. I suppose you mean mine. But as to my own blood, I will be responsible for that. One thing I know — whether blood will be shed or not, and I do not believe it will — I will not compromise with the savage rites."

When Legaic heard that his request had been refused, he begged the captain to ask for even a two-week vacation, but the captain told him it would be of no use to speak to Duncan again.

On December 20th, the day the girl was expected to return from the moon, Chief Legaic's wife hailed Duncan as he approached the schoolhouse. She informed him that all the chiefs were at her house and had sent her to ask him to close school for just that one day. But Duncan firmly answered, "No, not even for one hour."

"Then could you just not ring the bell today?" implored the chief's wife.

"No, I cannot do that. If I did not ring the bell the students would think there was no school today."

"Well, could you ring it softly, not so hard?"

"No, if I ring it at all, I will have to ring it as usual, so they can hear it."

The chief's wife went away crying over her failure, and Duncan stepped into the schoolhouse and resolutely rang the bell.

Although the bell made more noise than usual that day, only about eighty students attended class. The morning passed uneventfully, but during the afternoon Duncan noticed several Indians led by Chief Legaic walking single file towards the school. A few wore masks and all were decked out in war paint and charms.

When the medicine men entered the schoolhouse, the students quickly ducked out. Duncan stood quietly at his desk with his arms folded as the Indians pressed toward him.

Chief Legaic began his tirade by scolding the missionary for not obeying him, to which Duncan replied that he obeyed God before any man. Legaic, who had been drinking, moved in closer and spoke more abusively to Duncan. Brandishing a fearsome dagger he reminded Duncan that he had killed men before. As he swung his knife around in the air his medicine man, Cushwat, egged him on by yelling, "If you have courage — kill him! Cut off his head — now! Give his head to me and I will kick it on the beach."

Legaic's pride was stung by the reference to his courage, and he swung his knife again, this time as if to make a thrust at Duncan, when suddenly his arm fell to his side as if paralyzed, and he backed off and slunk away. The frustrated medicine men were obliged to follow after him.

As Duncan sank down onto his bench, he noticed Clah right behind him. Unknown to Duncan, one of his students had quickly run to tell Clah the terrifying news. Instantly the loyal Clah had hidden a revolver under his blanket and crept into the schoolhouse. At the moment Chief Legaic lifted his knife to strike, Clah moved in behind Duncan and aimed to fire.

That night Chief Legaic's daughter returned from the moon. All the Indians had gathered on the beach to look for her when suddenly she appeared, coming around the point on a little raft. The maiden was welcomed home with a great feast and elaborate ceremonies in her honor. The celebration lasted many days, and when all the feasting, dancing and howling accompanying Chief Legaic's daughter's "coming out party" were over, it was just one day before Christmas.

11

ON CHRISTMAS DAY Duncan arose early with a great feeling of expectation. After the attempt on his life and the subsequent ceremonies in honor of Chief Legaic's daughter, he had felt so discouraged he had wondered whether to carry out his long planned for Christmas program. But now, on Christmas Day, the early morning fog bands suspended over the water slowly lifted, and Duncan's spirit rose with them. A distant shaft of sunlight broke through the overcast sky, and by the time he left the fort to walk to the schoolhouse the sun was fully out and shining — coloring the usually muted landscape in brilliant hues. The wet moss on the rocks and driftwood, and the pods of seaweed that snapped under his feet all glistened in shades of ocher, green and rusty red-violet. The majestic green mountains were streaked with shifting blue shadows, and lightly dusted on top with sparkling snow which had fallen during the night.

Duncan's students had invited their parents and friends to visit the school on Christmas Day, and two hundred were already gathered when Duncan arrived. An air of festivity filled the room such as he had never felt before.

Now, for the first time, Duncan attempted to speak to the Indians without first having written out his ideas. He explained to the Indians, to whom Sunday was "dress day" and Christmas Day, "great dress day," why Christians celebrated this day as one of great joy for all people — that God's Son was born on this day. He spoke again of the Love of God, and of His hatred of sin, and especially called their attention to the sin of drunkenness. As he spoke he could see that his words went home to the consciences of many for the first time. After his sermon he questioned the children on Bible verses they had learned in school.

Then, to the complete joy and astonishment of the visitors, Duncan pulled out his old accordion and accompanied the children's singing of two hymns translated into their own language. Over and over again the delighted audience persuaded the children to sing their two songs until the audience, too, had learned the words and music. Again and again they urged Duncan to play the songs until all were able to join in, and the schoolroom was filled with the sound of their musical voices ringing out in confident harmony with Duncan's accordion.

Looking back on that wonderful Christmas Day — his second in the Northwest and his first outside the fort — Duncan always felt it marked the true begin-

ning of his mission among the Indians.

Their exuberant response to the service gave him renewed inspiration and every Sunday thereafter he held the same kind of service in the schoolhouse. Hymns were sung with great spirit, a short address given to the people on simple truths, then a closing song and prayer.

Seeing how much the Tsimshians loved to sing, Duncan was inspired to work late into the night translating hymns into their own language. Singing also became a popular part of the schoolwork, and with new vigor Duncan divided his school into separate, smaller classes, finding he was able to make better progress in this way.

Every session of school was opened with a prayer and a short address on a passage from the Bible. Then he had the students learn a text in English which he explained and paraphrased, and which they repeated again and again until it was firmly fixed in their minds.

The dismal winter rains once again whipped around the fort, but no longer confined within its walls and busy with his school, Duncan was oblivious to the constant dampness. Wearing a spruce root rain hat and a cedar-bark rain cape slung over his English coat, Duncan presented a novel sight in the wilderness as he strode down the beach to school.

Day after day Duncan went on teaching, and day after day the Indians became more and more interested. As the school and Sunday service took up their leisure time, they gradually had less and less time to indulge in their former Medicine Club work which was at its most feverish peak during the winter months. Week by week there were fewer who came to school painted in the savage style or with ornaments in their noses or lips. The drunken brawls in the camp also seemed to be slightly less fervent.

By March an important milestone was reached. At a council meeting held by the chiefs in Legaic's house it was resolved to send word to Duncan that they hoped he would keep on to "speak strong" against the bad ways of their people, and that they would support him with "strong speeches."

In April, when the Indians returned from the Nass River Oolakan fishing, a new student appeared at the schoolhouse. It was Chief Legaic. The head chief came not to cause trouble, but to sit and learn from the young white teacher. Legaic's attendance at school aroused great excitement in the camp. The prestige of Duncan's school grew rapidly, and his ministry gained in momentum as other chiefs soon followed Legaic's example and showed up in the classroom.

Only the disgusted medicine men resisted his teaching, but with Duncan's impressive new position in the Indian village, they were too fearful to instigate another attempt on his life. Instead they secretly vowed to evoke all their powers of magic against him, and to tempt and taunt the eager students away from the school.

12

IN SPITE of his loyal following, Duncan's life was still in danger as he moved among the Tsimshians, the danger sometimes erupting from the most innocent occasions. Noticing that his youngest students did not laugh or play, Duncan determined to give them some fun as well as instruction. With the older students' help he cleared a level strip of land behind the school and made a playground. From one of the felled trees they made a tall smooth pole, greased it well with Oolakan oil and tied a rain hat on top. When the greased pole was erected the children saw its purpose immediately, and everyone eagerly awaited his turn to try to climb the slippery pole and snatch the cap on top. This contest caused such an excited commotion that the older people, as well as little children too young for school, soon gathered around to watch the fun.

Seeing that the little ones were getting chilly standing there, Duncan spontaneously proposed that they run after him, and to the one who could catch him, he promised a piece of soap. As they all started to chase him, one child stumbled and fell. The others laughed at his clumsiness and the child began to cry. Immediately there was a skirmish in the crowd and a gun went off. The child's father, furious that his child had been "shamed," used the Indian logic that it would not have happened had not Duncan asked them to run after him. Pointing his gun at Duncan, he would have fired had not someone quickly grabbed hold of the muzzle of the gun, pushed it to the ground where it fired harmlessly, and held it there until the other Indians could disarm the outraged man.

Aware of this potential danger, Duncan nevertheless began to travel greater distances from the fort. That summer he bought and outfitted a seagoing canoe. Using caution, he selected only trustworthy boys from his school for paddlers and when a navigator was necessary, he made a point to choose an old man whom he could reasonably hope to overpower if attacked during the night's camp-out.

It was out on the water that Duncan found the greatest joy in the northland wilderness. The tangled underbrush of the forest made exploring by land a wet, weary struggle, but gliding over the water in a graceful canoe, progress was swift and exhilarating. Duncan's canoe, about twenty-five feet long by five feet wide, rose lightly over any waves likely to be met on the inside channels, and was easily paddled alongshore against moderate winds.

Scudding before a stiff breeze with two square ce-dar-bark sails up, the three young paddlers sometimes had nothing to do but chant the ancient canoe songs.

There were endless secret coves to explore, and so silently could the Indians dip their paddles that Dun-can could watch unnoticed the tussling of bears along the shore, and occasionally, the rare sight of frolicking sea otters. Offshore, there were other surprises in view: glittering black cormorants, when resting from fishing, had a habit of riding along on drifting logs and debris; and the most spectacular water bird, the great blue heron, was sometimes seen mingling with the ra-vens and eagles at the lower reaches of salmon streams.

Only a few yards back from shore the forest was as remote as ever, but the edge of the woods was inviting and accessible with snug harbors and beaches of dark sand where a canoe could be safely pulled up for the night.

Very little effort was required to make a comfortable campsite. It was only necessary to build a driftwood fire and spread out a blanket on moss two feet deep beneath hospitable spruce trees. On rainy nights they speedily set up shelters of cedar-bark matting over poles. The rain heightened the fragrance from the drenched trees, the wind played a wild melody in their top branches, and all the dripping wilderness was a soothing night song to Duncan in his little waterproof hut.

It was not until the following spring, in 1860, feeling confident that he now had the trust of many Indians, that he dared attempt the longer journey to the Nass River fishing grounds. Although only a few Tsimshians had more than a glimmer of real understanding, at least most of them had lost their dangerous superstitious attitude about him, and he felt he would be safe among them — the only white man among thousands of Indians.

Arriving at the Nass River before the run began, the Fort Simpson Tsimshians entertained the Nass River tribes with a Peace Dance which was designed to effect cordial relations among all the tribes sharing the fishing grounds. The chiefs themselves danced the Peace Dance, scattering eagle feathers and down over the heads of the crowd in the usual gesture of friendship.

While these festivities were under way, seal hunters were cruising out beyond the mouth of the river in attempts to find the first traces of the Oolakan. Several times a day a hair seal would be speared and its stomach opened for signs of the candlefish. As soon as this was noted, the festivities ceased, and all families made ready for the work which they knew would begin within a few days.

Now at last, Duncan was able to view with his own eyes the fabulous sight of the Oolakan run — the little candlefish so vital to the Tsimshian economy.

The little fish, about nine to twelve inches long, looked like a smelt. In the frying pan it melted away like a lump of butter, but when dried and provided with a wick, it burned like a candle.

By the middle of March millions of the little fish had come through Portland Inlet and were hustling over the bar of the Nass River. Along the banks and out on the river, thousands of Indians, all crying and yelling, "You are all chiefs, every one of you," attempted to fill their canoes with the shining, silvery fish. Using nets, baskets and even bare hands, everyone scooped up the slippery candlefish.

Out on the bar the canoes were steadied against the swirls and eddies of the river and strong downstream winds by three or more paddlers while at least two men combed the waters with a fish rake — a long shaft fitted with sharp bone teeth for two or three feet along one end. The rake was swept through the water, the

fish being impaled on the points from which they could be shaken off into the canoe.

Sea gulls by the thousands circled and dipped over the canoes, jabbering and mewing, then swooping down to catch their own supply of fish, sometimes managing to steal a fish directly from the end of a fish rake.

As the hordes of fish came swimming up the river, they were followed by great numbers of hungry sea mammals. Seals, porpoises, sea lions, and even killer whales churned the waters in pursuit, while the air above was filled with screaming flocks of gulls, crows, ducks and eagles.

Since each household required five to ten tons of fish to see them through the winter, the work continued almost without rest for the duration of the run. As the tons of fish were raked out of the water, they were carried away in large spruce root baskets and piled in heaps on the cooking sites where they were allowed to decompose partially before the cooking process began. The utmost care was taken not to offend the spirit of the candlefish, and for this reason the first caught were treated with great ceremony.

First a special woman was chosen. She had to be middle-aged and very dignified and solemn. For this occasion she wore a large spruce root hat and mitts on her hands. About fifty candlefish were brought to her and placed on a wooden rack over a special fire made of spruce bark. It was important that this fire must not be blown while the fish were cooking over it, for then a north wind might come roaring down the Nass River and upset the canoes.

As soon as the fish were nicely browned they were placed on a clean cedar mat and the woman divided them among the Indians partaking of the ceremony. All the Indians gave a big shout, exclaiming, "Lowaa," which means "great honor to the Oolakan." Each fish was held flat in the hand and eaten very hot. No one was allowed to cool it by blowing on it with his breath, for this would surely bring a storm. After eating the fish, no one, however thirsty he might be, was allowed to drink a drop of water. That would cause rain to fall and spoil the fishing.

Once this ceremony was over, thousands and thousands of bushels of fish were put into huge wooden vessels of water, made to boil by dropping in red-hot stones. After the grease from the boiling fish had been skimmed off, the remainder of the fish were scooped into rough willow baskets and the grease squeezed out of the boiling hot mass. Everyone, young and old, was busy with some phase of this activity. The women and children took charge of stringing the fish and hanging them to dry, while young boys cut firewood and helped make storage boxes for the Oolakan grease.

Tribes from far up the Nass River came to the fishing grounds at the mouth of the river both to fish and to trade with the coastal Tsimshians. Duncan was able to speak with some of these tribes, and word of the white man's school at Fort Simpson began to spread. Tales of his wonderful influence eventually penetrated into the interior, filling the savage hearts with awe and wonderment.

With the end of the Oolakan run the Indians returned to Fort Simpson to prepare for the hectic summer season of fishing, berrying and preserving. Schools of halibut were soon sighted in the ocean, and following that, the red salmon again began their annual run up the rapids of the Skeena River.

With the village once again partially deserted, Duncan closed the schoolhouse for the summer, and prepared for his first trip "outside" since his arrival three years before. It seemed like a good time to go; besides, Governor Douglas had sent word on the spring trip of the *Otter* that he would welcome a visit from Duncan. He had heard of the splendid work begun at Fort Simpson, and wanted Duncan's help in organizing a plan to Christianize the Indians in the camps outside Victoria, who were becoming more uncontrollable daily, especially as the liquor traffic increased.

Victoria was not the same placid hamlet Duncan had left three years before. The gold rush of 1858 had made many changes. The woodland path from Esquimalt to Victoria had grown to a bumpy road with the intervening space appropriated by thousands of Indians from Nootka Sound, and by human waifs left over from the gold rush. At every turn Duncan encountered a pandemonium of illicit traffic, stolen goods and frenzied drunkenness. The Hudson's Bay Company's exclusive license to trade in the Northwest Territory had been revoked, thus throwing the country open to the settlers who had gathered there from all over the world. The white population had grown to about three thousand. The old fort had been vacated, and gradually began to crumble into decay, but the little town of Victoria was on the first step of the way to becoming the major city of Western Canada in the nineteenth century.

That Governor Douglas had his hands full was obvious. Not only was he responsible for Victoria and Vancouver Island, but also for maintaining law and order on the mainland — in the Cariboo mining country along the Fraser River. As Governor of Vancouver Island, and now as Governor of British Columbia as well, Sir Douglas was the most important figure in the Northwest's early history.

Duncan was warmly welcomed by the governor, the Reverend Cridge and other friends who had held out little hope of ever seeing him again. During his stay he made detailed plans, approved by the government authorities, for helping the Victoria Indians. Could he have carried them out himself, they might have succeeded. But the people left in charge lacked the necessary patience and wisdom and soon abandoned the project as hopeless.

When he left again for the Northland in September, Governor Douglas gave Duncan the legal authority to warn all the Northern British Columbia Indians to keep their women away from Victoria. In order to carry out this assignment, and also because he had long desired to make the canoe trip to the Upper Nass River tribes, Duncan immediately began preparations for this journey. Since the currents in the Nass River were swift and treacherous, Duncan knew he could not expect to make the trip safely with only his young scholars for paddlers. Unless a strong man, experienced with the eddies of the river, was at the helm, it would be impossible to make much headway. Duncan therefore gratefully accepted the offer of Chief Kintsadah to pilot his canoe on the long trip upstream.

Arriving upriver, they had no sooner made camp on the bank when messengers from the chief arrived, inviting Duncan to attend a dance in his honor. Duncan refused, saying, "Tell him I did not come here to see dancing and I cannot go."

The messengers retreated but soon returned with word from the chief: "Tell the white chief he must come; if he doesn't come to me I won't go to hear his word; but if he will come I will go and listen to him."

Duncan was uncertain what to do — the idea, a missionary deliberately attending a savage ritual dance — how would he explain that? Consulting with his crew he was advised to go; if he did not go the chief would be offended. Duncan decided he had better give in for once, and he and his crew went along to the chief's house.

Upon entering the huge room, similar to chiefs' houses along the coast, Duncan was ceremoniously escorted to a seat of honor — an elaborately carved and painted wooden backrest with a bearskin robe spread in front of it. Facing a sail hung as a stage curtain, Duncan seated himself stiffly, deciding he would at least maintain a stern countenance during the savage performance.

Presently a beautifully costumed Indian holding a long staff stepped out in front of the curtain and, making a bow to Duncan, said, "Welcome, chief."

Then a second Indian appeared and began to chant, "Are the heavens going to change the hearts of our old men now?"

"Perhaps so, perhaps so," answered the other, striking time with his staff.

A group of Indians seated alongside the stage fell in with the chant, asserting in unison that the heavens were going to change the hearts of their people. As they solemnly chanted, the curtain was drawn aside, and there stood the young chief, dazzlingly arrayed in his ceremonial costume. With graceful motions he slowly stepped forward and saluted Duncan. Then looking up at the patch of sky showing through the smoke-hole, he chanted in his melodious language: "Great Father! Great Father of Heaven! You have sent Your Letter. Your Letter has reached this place. We, Your children here, are wanting it. Your servant has come here with it. Help him to teach us and we will listen. This chief has come to tell us about You. It is good, Great Father, we will hear."

As he continued his plaintive chant, all the while dancing in solemn measured steps, the choir now and then fell in, clapping their hands and repeating what he had sung.

Duncan was astonished — this was no savage dance — this was an eloquent prayer set to music and motion. The grace and beauty of their rhythmic chant melted Duncan's heart, and a great wave of tenderness for these Indians engulfed him.

Later in the day, as they had promised, the whole village came to his tent to listen while he spoke and sang to them, his crew joining in with the singing of hymns. The next day many of the men came to him and asked him to write out, so they could preserve it and look at it, a pledge against drinking intoxicating liquor. To his own pledge each Indian carefully signed his own mark, folded it carefully and took it away with him. This was undoubtedly the first temperance meeting ever held on the banks of the Nass River.

On the return trip downstream Duncan was lost in thought, pondering the spectacular reception given him. He had found it a profoundly inspiring experience. Contemplating the ritual of the English Church service, he questioned whether any civilized congregation could offer a more sincere and beautiful expression of worship than he had just witnessed. Duncan sensed the depth of the savage man's vague longing to uplift himself. More than ever it verified his conviction that the Indian, holding within him the same spark of humanity, longed to be treated as the white man's brother. He longed to be treated as an equal man. It was not his mentality that held him back, but only the quality of his experience. Duncan vowed that, with God's help, he would find the way to bring them that quality in lasting measure.

Duncan candidly realized that his successful results with the Indians were so far largely due to the impact of his own forceful personality. But to uphold "William Duncan" was not his purpose. He wanted them to have a faith in God that would sustain them in any situation, against any temptation. What he wanted for the Indians were permanent results that would long outlive his own time among them.

By the time they had crossed the bar at the mouth of

the river and were paddling southwest in Portland Inlet, Duncan had formulated a new plan — a daring
maneuver which would require serious and detailed
study — but one that would ultimately bring him
closer to his purpose. For the remainder of the journey
home these thoughts completely engrossed his mind.

13

THE WINTER RAINS came early in the fall of 1860. Following his return from the Nass River, Duncan opened school for the third year. But his students had barely settled into the routine of study when the westerly wind again swept down from the Arctic. The wet storms rolled in on the long swells from the North Pacific, driving salt spray and fog deep into the dark, saturated forest. Rain streamed down the furrowed bark of the giant trees, splashing glittering drops on the broad leaves of skunk cabbage and devil's club. Under all the dripping trees the mosses were more vibrantly green and lush than ever, making a soft cushion under the bellies of the martens and minks. As the black bears shuffled off into their dens to sleep out the winter, the lively blacktail deer came bounding down the mountain slopes to browse among the wet huckleberry bushes that grew higher than their heads.

All through that rainy fall and winter Duncan went on teaching the Tsimshians, each day reaching out to more and more of them. Although he severely attacked their savage rites, he did not ridicule their ancestral family customs nor speak against them unnecessarily. Nor did he offend the proud Tsimshians' sense of dignity. He simply went on teaching them — giving them light — and as the light began to grow, their works of greatest darkness began to disappear. The savage rites began to lose their hold on them, and finally, for his dedicated students, simply dwindled away altogether.

By January black bear cubs were born in the winter dens, and tiny pointed sprouts of new skunk cabbage, the bears' favorite root, began to push up through the damp sod to be ready for their springtime appetites.

To celebrate the New Year a school feast was held. More than two hundred and fifty Indians gathered to make speeches, sing songs and play games. The bulging schoolhouse was altogether too small for this occa-

sion, so definite preparations were made to build a new one in the spring. This time the Indians donated not only their labor but also helped pay for the new school.

At the first Sunday service in the new building over four hundred Indians attended, the biggest congregation of Indians Duncan had ever gathered together.

For a long time now Duncan had held classes twice a week for those who planned to be baptized into the Christian faith. By spring, nineteen adults and four children were ready. Only children of Christian parents were accepted. On the fringes were others who were eligible but, fearful of revenge from their still fierce relatives, dared not join them. Others who thought they were ready were advised by Duncan to wait until their comprehension was more advanced.

By keeping the applicants for baptism under a lengthy probation, he carefully protected the sacrament from turning into a magical rite. He did not want any Indians baptized who would invest the symbolic Christian ceremony with powers it did not possess. Nor did he intend to baptize great numbers of natives just to impress London in his reports.

He knew the Indians' fondness for singing — even the fiercest medicine man enjoyed singing hymns — and he knew their fondness for tobacco; for a few hours of singing and a pipeful of tobacco apiece he could have baptized all nine tribes!

Since Duncan was not a clergyman, he invited an ordained man to come to Fort Simpson to perform the sacrament. With skepticism a bishop came up from Victoria, but after questioning each Indian, his misgivings soon vanished.

The serious countenance of the Indian applicant was an impressive sight. In the dim glow of the schoolhouse lantern his native features were dramatized: his tawny face and high cheekbones; the glossy black flowing hair; the dark oval eyes; but the intensity in his solemn face was not of savage origin. The response of the Indian convert was intelligent and decisive as he declared in his own expressive tongue his readiness to worship and serve God.

Duncan rejoiced in the new Indians. How well he recalled that other June day over three years ago, when he had first spoken to them. How alone he had felt that night with the harsh realization that none had responded, none had understood. But now there was an aspiration toward a better way of life. Now he was no longer alone in the wilderness; he had loyal comrades to join him in praise to God for all that had been accomplished.

But Duncan's joy was soon darkened by the ridicule and temptations to which his new converts were subjected. It was especially difficult for the young people to remain steadfast in their new Christian faith when they were continually exposed to the taunts of their relatives. Particularly did he despair when any of these young people fell back into the old savage ways. Most frustrating of all was the realization that their downfall usually resulted from intoxicating liquor, and the liquor of course came from the white seagoing traders. Even the Hudson's Bay Company officials at the fort could not control the actions of all these men, for with increasing frequency the trading schooners appeared at Fort Simpson.

One morning on his way to the schoolhouse Duncan noticed two ships at anchor in the harbor, one flying an American flag, the other a Russian flag. When taking roll call he found that Wah-Tee-Boo, a young girl of thirteen, was absent.

"Where is Wah-Tee-Boo today? Is she sick?" asked Duncan, for the girl was one of his best students and helped him with the smaller children. The others did not seem to know.

After school Duncan walked down the far end of the beach to Wah-Tee-Boo's home. "Is Wah-Tee-Boo sick?" Duncan asked her old uncle, for the girl's parents were dead and she lived with her mother's relatives.

"No, she is not sick," answered the Indian, and turned away from Duncan as if to end the conversation.

"Well, where has she gone then?"

A scuffling and undertone of whispering among the Indians standing nearby suddenly made Duncan suspicious.

"What has happened to Wah-Tee-Boo?" Duncan demanded of all of them.

There was more whispering; then the old uncle finally answered, "The Russian traders bought her. They are taking her to Victoria."

"No, no," cried Duncan in anguish. "Don't you know what you have done?"

Not waiting to lash out at the old Indian further, he bolted out of the house and scanned the harbor. The Russian schooner was gone! Duncan ran back the length of the beach until he reached the canoe landing. Seeing several Indians working on a canoe, he called out, "How long ago did the Russians leave? . . . Good! With sails up we should make it — the wind is in our favor. You, Leht, get my canoe ready while I run for my money bag and coat. Get three more paddlers if you can find them quickly."

When Duncan came sprinting back to the beach, the canoe, with sails up, was ready to push off. Duncan scrambled into the stern, and sailing swiftly before a stiff wind, they were soon out of the harbor and shooting down the passage between the mainland and Finlayson Island.

In a few hours they sighted the schooner, and in another hour they overtook her just as she headed southwest toward Chatham Sound. The canoe came alongside, the crew yelling for attention, and in a few minutes Duncan was hoisted aboard. He did not waste pointless time chiding the Russians, but quickly bought back his young student.

The next day, however, Wah-Tee-Boo's relatives had a tongue-lashing from Duncan they were not soon to forget.

Episodes such as this, and worse, made Duncan determined to reveal the plan he had formulated sailing down the Nass River a year ago. As he saw it, he no longer had any choice but to remove his loyal followers from their present surroundings. He decided to broach the subject at the next church meeting. Just before he did so, however, an old chief surprised him by voicing these same ideas. "If you really want to make these children both good and happy," stated the wise old chief, "then you will have to take them away from here."

From then on Duncan insistently urged upon his

followers the necessity for moving to a new location where they could start a village of their own, a model Christian village where they could keep intoxicating liquors entirely away; worship God in their simple manner without fear of revenge from scoffers; and observe the Sabbath Day as became the true followers of the Christian faith.

1 4

THE CHRISTIAN INDIANS and the others who came regularly to Duncan's school and services were soon convinced that they must move away from the vicinity of Fort Simpson. Once the momentous decision was made, the big question was — what place would they choose for their new home?

At first there was a confusion of suggestions, but after many scouting trips the choice narrowed down to three or four likely locations.

One of these already had a name: it was called "Metlakatla," which means "an inlet with an outlet," or a through passage running parallel with the sea. Metlakatla, about seventeen miles south of Fort Simpson, was the original site of their ancestral village which had been abandoned after 1834 for the convenience of living near Fort Simpson, the center of trade and supply.

Duncan first inspected Metlakatla on one of those days when the entire landscape appeared to be in a state of fluid motion. Luminous shining currents streaked across the water; unrestricted swirls and strips of clouds shifted about in the sky, and the forested shoreline was only barely anchored and made tangible by the overlapping headlands and islands.

As they glided into the inlet the nearest islands were almost black in shadow, so dark and rich were the varying shades of green. The still water in little coves mirrored the dark shoreline, while high above the dense forest the snowcapped back ranges trailed off into a blur of ragged clouds. The deep stillness was broken only by the sounds of birds: ravens swooped and cawed among the treetops; gulls circled offshore; and sandpipers and curlews darted back and forth along the water's edge. Noting the sandy beach, Duncan knew it would furnish an excellent landing place for canoes. The harbor was well protected and there were portions of land on the promontories that, having once been cleared of the giant trees, would furnish fine garden spots for the new colonists.

Metlakatla was decided upon at the next meeting. The enthusiasm of the little band of pilgrims was so catching as they eagerly discussed their plans that many others began to find the idea appealing. But Duncan had no intention of taking along the half-hearted. It was to be a clean break with the past, and the requirements were so severe that many who were interested could not make the grade.

Duncan had methodically drafted a set of rules to

which each adult was obliged to pledge faithful allegiance before he could become a member of the future village. The rules were very definite:

1. To give up their medicine club work
2. To cease calling in the medicine man when ill
3. To cease gambling
4. To cease giving away their property for display and rank
5. To cease painting their faces
6. To cease drinking intoxicating liquor
7. To rest on the Sabbath
8. To attend religious instruction
9. To send their children to school
10. To be clean
11. To be peaceful
12. To be industrious
13. To be liberal and honest in trade
14. To build neat houses
15. To pay the village tax

To a civilized man the rules might seem simple enough, but to the Indian the first five rules alone required the surrender of all his ancient rituals. The drastic change from tribal life — with its sense of wholeness, its mystical bonds with nature — to the lonelier, more responsible life of civilization would be a severe test of individual endurance for the Indian. But Duncan had no idea of making the change an

easy one for anyone; no compromise with the past
could be tolerated in the new village.

All through the winter the pilgrims continued their
preparations for moving. The ground selected for the
site of the village was drained and cleared. By spring
of 1862 they were ready to go. The big schoolhouse,
probably the first prefabricated house in the wilderness, was carefully dismantled in sections, loaded onto
a raft and floated south to Metlakatla. The Indians
who went along with the raft planted potatoes and
started setting up temporary bark huts for the pioneers.

On an afternoon toward the end of May the pioneers started off. Heavy fog blurred the forest, and a
fine mist of rain fell silently on the calm water. Only

an occasional word among the men loading the canoes broke the awesome stillness. There was no sound from the Indians who lined the beach to watch the departure. With anxious faces they watched the six canoes resolutely push off for Metlakatla. Scanning the solemn faces before him, Duncan felt a great surge of compassion for his little group of fifty. He knew he was beginning an eventful page in the history of the Tsimshian people.

15

From the moment the six canoes scraped gravel on
the beach at Metlakatla, William Duncan felt a great
new surge of energy and dedication. All the loneliness
and frustrations of the past five years seemed to wash
away from him like so much seaweed on an ebb tide.
Ahead lay mile after mile of unspoiled, uninhabited
forest land, and the glorious opportunity to create a
new kind of life out of the wilderness.

Sharing their leader's zeal, the little group of pioneers set to work clearing and building. With the huge
logs from the felled trees they began to build permanent houses, but meanwhile they lived in huts of cedar-
bark matting.

At the end of each day's work they gathered on the
shore for singing and evening prayer, but before the
long June twilight had faded into night everyone was
asleep.

Everyone, that is, except Duncan, who lingered on
to enjoy the luxury of being out at night — alone and
safe. Not in all his five years at Fort Simpson had he

dared indulge his inclination to walk alone at night. Now for a long time he watched while the pale evening light cast sky and water in a silvery iridescence, diminishing the details of mountains and islands to a transparent haze of violet. Very slowly the water darkened until only slivers of light edged the merging of forest and sea. It was midnight before the light faded completely, and the shadowy mountains turned to black shapes against the starry sky. The summer wind whistled softly on the wings of the night birds, and soon the sky was filled with the rustle of their flight to the Arctic. Not until his eyes closed in fatigue could Duncan bear to give up the beauty of the northern summer night.

About two weeks later Duncan noticed dark specks on the overcast horizon. Scanning the gray water again, he saw the specks grow bigger, until at closer range they became canoes — thirty long war canoes, dashing down the inlet toward Metlakatla. As they skimmed across to the landing beach Duncan saw that they held about three hundred Tsimshians and all their belongings — almost the whole Kitlahn tribe, including their chief. There was great rejoicing as the pioneers greeted relatives and friends, and in one joyful scrambled moment the tiny community tripled in population.

Immediately more land was cleared, more buildings started and garden plots established.

Keeping law and order among the Indians and all their activity required all of Duncan's executive powers. But he was well prepared. He had long ago mapped out all the details for managing his model community, and now he set them into action. There were to be no chiefs in Metlakatla. Unless the old tribal system was broken up, Duncan knew the new life could never take hold. The government of the new village was completely in his hands, which was the only way he could keep order in the beginning.

His only assistants were twelve native constables, chosen by him, who saw that peace was maintained, that no strangers coming among them misbehaved, and that the people lived up to the agreed-upon rules.

Later on the number of constables was increased to thirty and a village council appointed, also handpicked by Duncan. To this group he gave an advisory voice in village affairs, but reserved to himself the final decisions in all matters.

Still later, when their minds had more readily grasped civilized ways, he taught them how to elect their own village council members.

Since few of the Indians could write, it was necessary to cast ballot by other methods, most of which proved too slow. Finally they found a way in which ten men could be elected in half an hour. The electors stood up, facing a wall. When a man was nominated, any person opposed to him put his closed fist behind his back. If in favor, the hand was open. Sometimes Duncan, who was the sole judge of the election, saw a closed fist move violently behind a back. Ten or more closed fists defeated the candidate.

All through the summer fishing season the Indians who had remained behind in the village continued the clearing and building. By fall of 1862 the village had thirty-five houses, each eighteen by thirty-four feet. Governor Douglas had furnished the nails and windows for each house. Duncan's log house contained a sitting room, kitchen and bedroom. Still being built, with the hope it would be finished for their first Christmas, was a large octagonal church which was to hold seven hundred people. The church had no flooring except gravel, and two huge fireplaces with the Indian style smoke-holes above.

By New Year's Day of 1863 the residents of Metlakatla were ready to pay their first annual village tax: one blanket or $2.50 for every adult male; and one shirt or $1 for every boy approaching manhood. The proceeds were to be used toward village improvements — that year for the building of a planked walk around the village. The total tax collection was: one green, one blue, and ninety-four white blankets; one pair of white trousers; one dressed elk skin; seventeen shirts; and $7.

As Metlakatla entered the New Year, its fame began to spread. More and more was it becoming a haven of hope to those Indians discerning enough to foresee the decline of their own people. Hardly a week went by but another canoe swept down the inlet with new pioneers. Most of all was it a refuge to the slaves of the ruling class, for to escape to Metlakatla meant freedom forever. Occasionally a canoe was sighted drifting aimlessly in the inlet. Upon investigation the Indians would find a slave slumped in the bottom, too starved and exhausted to paddle the rest of the way to shore. With great tenderness these poor people were helped into the houses at Metlakatla and cared for until their strength returned.

One day a particularly impressive war canoe came skimming down the inlet. As the canoe gracefully turned in toward the landing beach Duncan could see it was elaborately carved and decorated, indicating the crest of a chief. Duncan shook his head in disbelief as the three vague figures came into focus — Chief Legaic, his wife and daughter. The three were doing their own paddling.

Duncan vividly recalled his first sight of Chief Legaic five years before. Then, too, he had approached by canoe, but in such different style — standing majestically in the stern, the canoe paddled by many slaves.

Now Chief Legaic wore no ceremonial regalia, and he deftly beached his own canoe above the high tide line. Only his proud dignity was the same as he walked up the beach toward Duncan and solemnly began to speak.

"A few years ago the other chiefs and I decided we wanted our people to learn the white man's knowledge from you. Compared with the white man's knowledge, we are only blind children, knowing not how best to live, either here or in the country we go to after we die. And so I wished for my people to learn new ways from you, and to teach it to their children.

"Until you came, the only white men we had met wanted to get something from us. They all seemed to be seeking their own good — not our good. Until you came, you might say that all my life I have never heard a white man speak. It has always seemed to me that trying to speak to traders was like speaking to a person across a broad stream that was running fast over stones and making so loud a noise that scarce a single word could be heard. But now the Indian and the white man are on the same side of the river, eye to eye, heart to heart.

"I have always loved my people. I have stayed with them because a chief never deserts even his bad and foolish people in times of trouble. But since you left Fort Simpson the bad ways of the white men bring even greater misery to my tribes. More and more have gone bad on whiskey; hundreds more have died from the smallpox disease. I have taught them and ministered to them as well as I could, but hereafter I will keep silent and listen to your words. By my own example, I hope that all the people will listen and follow men here."

Then, as a symbol of his word, the chief presented Duncan with a bone dagger, the handle superbly carved to represent the head of a bear, and crouched between the bear's ears, the figure of a man. It was the same dagger he had pointed at Duncan five years before.

Duncan was impressed and surprised by Chief Legaic's speech. He shook his hand and assured him that he and any of his people who sincerely promised to follow the regulations of the village were welcome. But his warm greeting was not without apprehension, for Chief Legaic, in attempting the new life, had more of the power, prestige and advantages of the old to relinquish than any other Tsimshian. In Metlakatla inherited rank and chieftanship stood for nothing. Only by individual endeavor and character could a man rise to leadership. For Chief Legaic, Duncan foresaw a long frustrating struggle, but that day he optimistically led him into the heart of the village.

16

Although Duncan insisted that the Tsimshians relinquish their tribal system when entering Metlakatla, he did not urge them to adopt civilized ways of living until they were ready for it. He felt strongly that they should be thoroughly educated up to every step before it was taken.

But Metlakatla was a place where knowledge and understanding thrived. An exciting spirit of progress seemed to fill the very atmosphere. It was not long before more and more of the Christian Tsimshians began to assume civilized ways naturally.

This created an ironic problem. When a Tsimshian Indian became a Christian, he also became poorer than when he was a heathen. To become a Christian did not make him a smarter hunter or a more skillful fisherman, but it did awaken his desire to improve himself in material ways. Previously, his old blanket sufficed for clothes. Now his wife needed a dress to wear to church, and his children needed clothes to wear to school. His expenses were rapidly rising, but his income remained the same.

Duncan had foreseen that this would happen, and he intended to show them evidence of material advantages to be gained in adopting the new life. At Highbury College Duncan had critically studied the techniques of the British missionaries to Africa and India. The mistake of many of the bishops sent there had been their refusal to acknowledge the practical qualities of primitive peoples while attempting their transformation solely through the rituals of the church. Duncan perceived that an Indian, like a small child, was full of cravings for possessing something he could not describe, and was a frail creature, needing to be fed with bread as well as food for the soul.

Therefore, Duncan, the practical businessman — the former young British executive — set about to open new sources of income to the Indians, as well as to encourage them to their utmost capacity in the time-honored industries they already had. Out of his own small allowance from the Missionary Society he paid the Indians wages for their work on his house, the church, and all public improvements such as walks, drainage and garden plots. He started a soap factory, making soap from Oolakan grease, which served the double purpose of inspiring cleanliness as well as creating steady employment for several people. He encouraged them to extraordinary efforts to secure furs for trading, to prepare smoked salmon, Oolakan grease and dried berries for shipment to Victoria.

But all this effort directed toward developing a civilized community created civilized problems. In order to export their goods and to buy the new necessities of life, they were obliged to go to Fort Simpson to trade with the Hudson's Bay Company agents, or to encourage the visits of the trading schooners. Either choice had disastrous results. Going to Fort Simpson exposed them to the very temptations from which Duncan had removed them. And the trading schooners were nothing but grog shops: their visits to Indian settlements were marked by murder and the maddest of riots.

Duncan asked the Hudson's Bay Company to open a branch trading post store in Metlakatla where the Indians could exchange furs for goods without going to the fort. The only conditions Duncan asked were that the agent in charge should be a decent man who would not in any way hinder the Christian and civilizing work being carried on; and that no intoxicating liquor be sold in the store.

But the company would not open a store in Metlakatla. And neither did they care to have anyone else do so. Although no longer holding an official monopoly on the fur trade, their influence was still powerful, especially in the wilderness areas.

Then Duncan managed to interest several Victoria merchants in his idea, but fearing repercussions from the Hudson's Bay Company, they reluctantly declined.

Duncan was not long daunted — he decided to open the store himself. He knew something about business, and he could buy the furs and other articles from the Indians himself and have them shipped to Victoria. With the money he had saved from his salary during his five years at Fort Simpson, he paid cash for a small stock of store goods and opened the shop for business.

Immediately he was faced with another problem. Metlakatla was six hundred miles from Victoria, and the only means of public transportation along the coast was the Hudson's Bay Company steamer. It had not occurred to him that they would refuse to carry his freight.

Duncan solved this problem by buying and outfitting his own schooner. He managed to borrow $500 from the British Columbia government and since he wanted the Indians to feel personally interested in the enterprise, he persuaded them to buy shares at $5 each, amounting to a total of $400. The balance he advanced from his own private funds. Soon the *Carolina,* with a native master and crew, was sailing up and down the coast, shipping furs by the ton.

As soon as the other Indians discovered that their furs brought higher prices at Duncan's store, they transferred their trade to Metlakatla. The Hudson's Bay Company had long underpaid the Indians in trade. Marten skins, at the fort, were only worth 25¢. Duncan paid $3 and $4 for them. Mink skins, instead of 2¢, were 50¢ and 85¢. And the rare sea otter pelts, instead of a shameful $10 or $12, brought a true value of $100. As a result, the *Carolina* now carried a full cargo both ways, and was kept busy running all the time.

At the close of the year Duncan paid each Indian

stockholder $5 per share in dividends. This they did not understand at all, and assumed they were giving up their interest in the schooner. When Duncan carefully explained to them, over and over again, that they still retained their interest, that the sum only represented what they had earned on their original investment, the Indians "died." After that they wanted to re-christen the schooner "Hah," meaning a "male slave," because "he does all the work and we get all the profits."

The powerful Hudson's Bay Company was annoyed with Duncan's success. Used to having their own way, they did not intend to stand for this interference with their business, especially not from a mere missionary. A plan was evolved that would soon crush this inconvenient young man. An order was given to overbid him on furs, and to undersell him on goods the Indians wanted to buy. If necessary, they knew they could afford to keep this up for a year.

Duncan immediately went to the fort. "I have heard what the company plans to do, and I am perfectly willing to have you carry out the orders. I do not fear you, and I will tell you frankly how I will act in the matter, so that you may take your measures accordingly.

"My goods are all paid for, and if I do not sell a thing it will not break me. The moment I hear that you have started to raise the price of furs over a fair living price, or that you have lowered the price of store goods below a fair profit, I will lock up my store. I will not sell another article, nor buy another fur. I will send all the Indians to you, and I will tell them they can make a splendid profit by coming to the fort.

"But, mind you, you will have to keep on with your plan and your prices. The moment I hear that you have come down again on furs, or gone up again on store goods, I will reopen my store and tell the Indians to come back and trade with me. These Indians have no feeling of loyalty for Fort Simpson, but they will do anything for me. They will do just as I tell them. What do you think about my plan?"

The company's order to overbid and undersell Duncan was revoked. For the first time in its history, the Hudson's Bay Company had to acknowledge a defeat in its great trade in Northwest Territory. Not only did the directors conclude that the best policy was not to balk Duncan in his little enterprise, but within six months they notified him that, if he desired to sell his own schooner, they would be able to ship his freight on their steamer. Receiving a cash price of $1,000 for the *Carolina*, Duncan was able to repay the loan to the government officials who were very surprised to receive payment from a poor missionary.

The profits from the successful trading store were applied to public improvements of all kinds, and to new enterprises which would furnish employment within the village. A blacksmith's shop was started and then a carpenter's shop. But the sawmill was the most exciting to the Indians. When the waterwheel was first placed in position and the sawmill started, the

Indians all "died" they were so amazed that water could be made to saw wood. For days they came and squatted by the mill, intently watching the marvelous operation.

There was no doubt as to the exciting economic success of the new village. As to its spiritual progress, Duncan wrote home to the Church Missionary Society:

About four hundred to six hundred souls attend divine services on Sundays and are being governed by Christian and civilized laws. About seventy adults and twenty children are already baptized, or are only waiting for a minister to come and baptize them. About one hundred children are attending the day school, and one hundred adults the evening school. . . .

The instruments of the medicine men, which have spellbound their nation for ages, have found their way into my house, and are most willingly and cheerfully given up. The dark and cruel mantle of heathenism has been rent, so that it can never be made whole.

Feasts are now characterized by order and goodwill, and begin and end with the offering of thanks to the Giver of all good gifts. Scarcely a soul remains away from divine service, excepting the sick, and their nurses. Evening family devotions are common in almost every house, and better than all, I have a hope that many have ex-

perienced a real change of heart. Thus the surrounding tribes have now a model village before them, acting as a powerful witness for the truth of the Gospel, shaming and correcting, yet still captivating them, for in it they see those good things which they and their forefathers have sought and labored for in vain — to wit: peace, security, order, honesty, and progress. To God be all the praise and glory!

Thus the little village steadily advanced into civilized life, each day gaining in strength and knowledge. But with every step forward, trouble and conflict kept even pace; their worst difficulties originating not from within the Indian community, but from the white man's world without.

17

Beyond the coastal mountains that isolated the Pacific Northwest from the rest of the continent, two giant young nations were steadily advancing westward. One had been slowed down by the turmoil of Civil War, but with the end of fighting in 1865, its momentum increased as stagecoaches and wagon trains raised their dust across the plains, then creaked their way over the mountains and down to the Pacific coast. Tracks laid for the first transcontinental railroad were finally completed in 1869, thus linking the United States from coast to coast. In Canada, the Pacific route lagged behind. Its tracks were still being laid across the continent, not to be completed until 1886 when the first train finally came thundering down the coastal mountains to meet the Pacific at the tiny hamlet of Vancouver, British Columbia.

But Canada was progressing in other ways during the '60's: without the armed struggle of Civil War and the violence of the Indian conflicts which accompanied America's growth, Canada was patiently advancing from one precarious step to another along the road to nationhood. In 1867 it was achieved. The four provinces of Nova Scotia, Quebec, New Brunswick and Ontario were united under the new name, "Dominion of Canada." But this first federation was only the beginning of the transcontinental domain upon which Canadian ambitions were fixed: to extend the new dominion from sea to sea was the compelling urge of the national leaders. Ahead stretched the vast prairies and mountains of the Northwest Territories, across which there was neither wagon road nor railway. And still farther west, on the Pacific coast, was the independent Province of British Columbia carrying on a life of its own, entirely separated from the rest of Canada.

As the heyday of the gold miners and fur trappers came to a close, "Timber!" became the big cry in both the American and Canadian Pacific Northwest. The coastal towns of Portland, Tacoma and Seattle developed rapidly during the '60's as practical, ambitious men saw the value of the mighty trees and began to cut them down.

In British Columbia the town of Victoria passed through several stages of growing pains. From a cluster of cabins huddled around Fort Victoria it had become a wild and booming gold rush town — the outfitting point for the Cariboo mining country. Its harbor was full of ships coming and going, leaving men of many nationalities in the streets. Thousands of people passed through and some stayed to buy land from the thrifty first settlers. Following the gold seekers came substantial settlers from England to try their luck in Victoria. The mild damp climate was pleasing to the English, and, seeing how profusely everything grew, they were encouraged to send home for seeds and slips of plants.

It was becoming increasingly difficult to administer the affairs of two growing colonies from two places — Victoria on the island and New Westminster on the mainland. Therefore, by royal proclamation in 1866, QueenVictoria united the colony of Vancouver Island with the mainland province, forming the one Crown Colony of British Columbia. Chosen as the capital of the united province, Victoria gradually began to assume the elegance appropriate to a dignified British government center.

Victoria also had visions of becoming the chief port of trade between America and the Orient, for there was a lively trade by sea up and down the coast with the ports of San Francisco, Portland and Seattle. Increasing numbers of ships set sail from all these ports, their captains seeking fortunes of one sort or another in the undeveloped far Northland. And from the opposite direction — from Sitka, Alaska — the Russians, in search of their fortunes, continued to sail the waters of the Inside Passage.

One of these sea traders was a sharp, unscrupulous man named Charles Baranovitch who was not particular about how he made his money. He was quite willing to get the best of the Indians in a fur trade by giving them "firewater," although he well knew it was not only against the law but also extremely dangerous, especially to any white men who might come their way while the Indians were under its influence.

Baranovitch had a fine schooner and traded all the way from Sitka to Victoria. When he sailed into the harbor at Metlakatla, it was rumored that he had liquor aboard. Duncan took to his canoe and paddled out to the ship, having first posted a large group of Indians on the beach to await a signal from him.

Duncan went aboard and informed Baranovitch that he had no objection to his trading with the Indians, as long as he did not sell them any liquor. He had heard, Duncan said, that Baranovitch was dealing in liquor, and before he allowed trading to begin, he wanted to search the schooner.

Baranovitch inquired of Duncan as to what authority he had for such action. Duncan replied, "Authority? I have no authority, sir, except the authority of self-defense. My life is in the hands of these Indians. They are my friends now. But if you take away their reason, I will have nothing with which to defend my life. And I am going to prevent your placing my life in jeopardy if I can."

"How are you going to prevent it?" Baranovitch asked.

"Do you see those Indians on the beach? They are only waiting for a signal from me. The moment they get it, they will rush aboard this ship, overpower your crew, beach your schooner and burn it with all its contents. They will do it at one word from me. Will you let me search your schooner peaceably, or shall I give those men the signal?"

Baranovitch consented, but nothing was found. If it was on board, it was well hidden away. Baranovitch solemnly agreed not to sell liquor to the Indians and shortly left. Later, in Victoria, he complained to Governor Douglas of the high-handed outrage to which Duncan had submitted him.

Governor Douglas wrote Duncan that he suspected he had taken the law into his own hands, but that he did not censure him for it. In order that he might not have to do it again, however, without having the legal authority with which to protect himself, the governor enclosed a commission appointing Duncan a magistrate with jurisdiction over five hundred miles of the coastline of British Columbia and all its hundreds of islands.

From his official "bench" Judge Duncan handed down some original and peculiar sentences not found in the statute books. In sentencing one whiskey seller, Duncan decreed: "I have the right to give you six months in jail, but as you claim that it is your first offense, and as I have never heard of you before, I will let you off with one month. But, since the jail is cold and I am not going to keep a fire going there for your sake, I will not order you to be confined in prison. Instead you shall go with the constable and live at his home for one month. If you disobey him, I will give him orders to put you in the jail at once."

As a legally appointed judge, Duncan was also better able to handle the Indian lawbreakers, although he did not always follow the strictest letter of the law. As he admitted, "I have sometimes gone a little outside of the law. I have never allowed myself to stumble over a law when something good was to be accomplished."

Thus, when an Indian was found guilty of an act of violence which could have resulted in murder, the sentence invariably was a public whipping. To the proud Tsimshians this was a most effective punishment since the entire village was summoned to witness the affair, generally administered by one of the constables. The public whipping also alleviated the Indian's savage instinct for revenge. In several cases the whipping probably saved the guilty man's life, as the man he had wronged, if still a heathen, would likely have taken his own revenge instead of publicly declaring himself satisfied with the official punishment.

For people who had only a few years ago idolized the power of rank and social position, an effective, nonviolent method for getting rid of an offender was by means of the "black flag." A tall flagstaff attached to the octagonal building in the center of the village flew the British flag on festive occasions, but when a wicked man was desired to leave town, Duncan hoisted the black flag, showing that a public enemy was in camp. In a few moments public opinion was aroused and tongues began to wag. It didn't take long before the identity of the offender was known to everyone. Not being able to tolerate the public scorn which the black flag indicated, the offender usually ducked out of town.

The black flag did not always succeed, however. Upon the death of his uncle, a new chief came into his rank as head of the Kitlahn tribe. Since many of the Kitlahns were living at Metlakatla, the new chief traveled there to call a secret meeting of the tribe. He told them how their old ancestral customs were being abolished; their proud memories and warlike traits disgraced; and he exhorted them to go back to the old feasts and joys. When Duncan heard of the secret meeting, he immediately ran up the black flag. But the chief refused to leave. Duncan walked out in front of his cabin with his revolver in hand, and standing where the chief could plainly see him, commanded the constables, "Go over and tell him for me that in ten minutes by the watch, his canoe is to be hauled down, and he on his way out. If not, I will meet him face to face. And one of us, perhaps both, will die." Inside of five minutes the chief's belongings were brought down to the beach, his canoe pushed off, and without further word he paddled off.

Through countless incidents and their solutions Duncan guided the Metlakatlans into the complexities of civilized life, and as their comprehension of law and order grew, he helped the Native Council and the police force to handle their own affairs competently.

During the last half of the 1860's Duncan was so engrossed with Metlakatla's affairs, he took little notice of events culminating both to the north and south —

events which would someday be of great significance to Duncan and the Indians. To the south, the Province of British Columbia was going through a difficult period of indecision with two radically opposing directions possible: either confederation with the new Dominion of Canada, or annexation to the United States.

The vigorous pioneers who were building civilization in the province were excited about the possibilities of their magnificent country, and they needed a more democratic government than that of a British colony — more opportunity for advancement. Geographically they were in easy communication with the Pacific states and enjoyed a growing connection with them. Many of the settlers who had come from the States were in favor of this solution, and in 1867 the annexationists petitioned the Colonial office for release from the British Empire. Two years later a petition was circulated for a request to President Grant to arrange the transfer of the colony to the United States. But the influence of those in favor of confederation was stronger, and finally, in 1871 British Columbia entered the Dominion of Canada.

Although the Russian-Alaskan boundary line was only thirty-five miles north of Metlakatla, Duncan knew even less of the affairs originating from that remote territory.

Russia's hold in Alaska had been gradually weakening. The peak of her influence had been reached way back in 1818 under Alexander Baranof. Ruling from the flourishing capital of Sitka, the Russians had for years dominated the fur trade. However, the British Hudson's Bay Company had gradually become more influential, finally extending its territory right up to the Russian boundary line. With more pressing problems at home, and realizing it was only a matter of time until they lost their vast North American possession to Great Britain, the Russians interested the United States government in purchasing it.

William H. Seward, Secretary of State under President Lincoln, was the key figure in the negotiations. With farsighted wisdom Seward realized that in order to defend the United States properly Alaska was needed to dominate the North Pacific. When the message was received that the Russians would agree to a sale price of $7,200,000 (less than 2¢ an acre), Seward made great haste to work out all the details, fearing that once the news leaked out, England might try to stall the sale until she could maneuver to get Alaska herself. Seward and Baron deStoeckl, the Russian Minister, worked all through the night to complete the transaction, and that is why the document was signed at the odd hour of 4 A.M., on March 30, 1867, in Washington, D.C.

The formal transfer to the United States took place in Sitka, Alaska, in October. It was a windy, overcast day. Heavy clouds moved swiftly across the dark mountains, now and then breaking to give a glimpse of the snowcapped peaks. Russian and American troops took up their positions before a ninety-foot flagpole on the parade grounds of the Russian castle. No Alaskan

natives were invited to the ceremony. The Indians, however, took to their canoes and from the harbor watched the proceedings with great interest. As the thirty-two cannons around the castle and the guns of the warships in the harbor boomed out in salute, the double eagle of Imperial Russia slowly fluttered down the pole. The American troops then moved in with the Stars and Stripes and sent it smartly to the top where the flag snapped in the wind, its bright colors gay against the dark sky. Now three symbols could be seen against Sitka's towering mountains, representing the three cultures which had shared in Alaska's history: the onion spire of Imperial Russia; the totem pole of the Alaska natives; and the brand new flag of the United States of America.

18

Cᴴɪᴇꜰ Lᴇɢᴀɪᴄ ᴡᴀs ᴅʏɪɴɢ. On his way home from the Nass River he was taken ill at Fort Simpson and now the former head chief of the Tsimshians was weakly penning a note to Duncan which would be sent along by canoe:

> Dear Sir, I want to see you. I always remember you in my mind. I shall be sorry not to see you before I go away, because you showed me the ladder that leads to heaven, and I am on that ladder now. I have nothing to trouble me, only I want to see you.

Accompanied by Clah, Duncan speedily set out for Fort Simpson by canoe. But Legaic had died before they arrived. Duncan was handed the last note written by Legaic:

> My Dear Sir, This is my last letter, to say I am going to rest from trouble, trial and temptation. I

don't feel afraid to meet my God. In my painful body I always remember . . .

But here the pen had fallen from the dying man's hand.

Duncan was comforted in knowing that this once proud and savage chief had died with a peaceful heart. It had not been easy for Legaic in the beginning. As head chief of the Tsimshian Nation, Legaic was continually invited back to Fort Simpson to attend a potlatch, feast, or initiation ceremony. As Duncan had feared, Legaic had a hard time giving up his chieftainship. He could not resist honoring these occasions by appearing in his full ceremonial regalia.

Duncan repeatedly advised him not to go: "You have to be one thing or the other." But Legaic wanted to belong to both sides. He really wanted to lead a good life at Metlakatla, but he also wanted to enjoy the prestige of the old. And sometimes his talk threatened to cause unrest among the Indians of Metlakatla.

Finally Duncan sent for him, saying, "Legaic, you had better leave here and go back to Fort Simpson. I don't want you here. You are wearing the mantle on both shoulders. You want to serve both God and the Devil and you are doing the Devil's work here. You had better leave here and go back, for your heart is there, where you can be a Chief."

About a week later Duncan heard a knock at the door of his cabin. It was late at night. When he opened the door, he found Legaic standing there. He quickly scanned Legaic's hands for a weapon, fearful that he had come back in the night for revenge.

"What do you want?" asked Duncan.

"I want to come in," answered Legaic.

"What do you want here?"

"I want to talk with you."

"All right. Come in then."

Legaic walked dejectedly into the room, his eyes cast down.

"So you have come back," Duncan said to him.

"I have come back."

"Why did you, when I told you to go away?"

"Because I could not help it. I have not slept for nights. I have come back to say to you: tell me what to do, and I will do it. There is only one thing you must not tell me to do, for I will not do it."

"What is that?" asked Duncan.

"Do not tell me to go away. I will not do it, for I cannot do it."

Impressed by his earnestness, Duncan allowed him to return. This time Legaic succeeded in overcoming the temptations of his former life. When he asked to be appointed a constable, his request was readily granted. The constables were highly respected in the village, and were furnished with a cap, belt and cape as badges of office. Perhaps this visible distinction helped Legaic make up for the loss of his chieftainship. About a year later, Legaic and his wife and daughter became Christians. At his baptism he took the name of Paul.

Duncan was distressed that he had not been able to reach Paul Legaic before he died, for the Indian had finally become one of his most able assistants and a loyal friend.

Now a new generation was growing up in Metlakatla, with a different background from that of Paul Legaic. These were the children who had started out in the very first school held in Chief Legaic's house. They had been taught and guided by Duncan all through their growing-up years, and now were civilized young men and women. They were Duncan's most loyal followers. He, in turn, dearly loved these young people; they were the object of his most tender and thoughtful concern.

Duncan knew these handsome, intelligent young Indians were capable of much more skillful work than could be found within the limits of Metlakatla. The spirit of improvement needed fresh material and knowledge in order to develop itself. If not found for them, Duncan knew they would be drawn to the settlements of the white people where he feared numbers of them would become victims of white men's vices and diseases.

With this in mind, Duncan decided the time had come to make his first trip home to England where he could inquire and learn about new trades and interests for Metlakatla. He had been in the northern wilderness for thirteen years, and, except for a few trips to Victoria, had never been long away from his mission. He knew he could trust them to handle their own

131

affairs during his absence, and that they would feel proud to be worthy of his confidence.

In January 1870, Duncan bid them all individual farewells, but after he had boarded the steamer they took to their canoes and followed along. Down the inlet they accompanied him until they reached the wide waters of Chatham Sound, all the while chanting English hymns in Tsimshian language. Sea gulls squawked and dipped over the canoes, and porpoises played and dove alongside the steamer. It was a gay farewell.

Duncan had a long list of projects for Metlakatla. He had jotted them down in his memo book: wool-teasing, carding, spinning, weaving, cleaning, dyeing, drying; making soap, brushes, baskets, rope, clogs, staves; dressing deerskins; making bricks; making tiles; gardening; photography; and music.

First he went to an old Irish woman who taught him how to spin. Then he went to Manchester to learn the processes of weaving wool, and on to Yarmouth to learn rope-making. He took volumes of notes and purchased various supplies, including a camera, photographic plates and chemicals.

Right from the beginning, Duncan had noticed that the Tsimshians had fine voices and a good ear for music, though their only instruments were their drums and rattles. Duncan was eager to bring them the instruments for a brass band, but when he inquired the price, he found it was far too high. The music dealer, however, told him of a wealthy silk manufacturer who, after purchasing thirty instruments for a brass band for his workmen, had got into some trouble with them over a strike, and now had the unused instruments locked up — perhaps he would sell them at a good discount.

Duncan called on this manufacturer. He told him about the Indian Mission, and that, if he could afford them, he would like to buy the instruments. The man listened with great interest to Duncan's story, but when he had finished, merely replied, "My instruments are not for sale, sir."

"Then I beg your pardon for intruding and taking up your time," said Duncan.

"I said they were not for sale. But that does not prevent my making you a present of them, does it? You may take them, and I hope you will have more joy from them than I have had."

On the return ocean trip Duncan stopped in San Francisco where he was able to buy a set of looms and other machinery for a weaving plant from a manufacturer who intended to put improved machinery into his own factory.

Finally he was back in Victoria again. Calling on a music teacher, he informed him he wished to learn to play all of his various instruments. The teacher exclaimed, "One man — the entire band? How much time do you have?"

"Only a little. I leave here in eight days for the North," replied Duncan.

"Impossible!" cried the distressed music teacher.

But this was a word Duncan did not comprehend. He paid the man $11, had eleven lessons, and learned enough about each instrument to give basic instruction to each Indian musician.

Also loaded onto the steamer at Victoria was an organ for the church, thus relieving his old accordion from public service.

Duncan arrived in Metlakatla a year after he had left. A long and splendid canoe hailed the steamer near the mouth of the Skeena River. He readily left the ship and proceeded the rest of the way home with his Indian friends, rejoicing anew at the sight of the familiar islands, and the sweep of the great headlands plunging into the sea.

There was a strong wind, and with two sails up, the canoe sped swiftly over the water. His happy friends, having nothing to do but sit still and watch the sails, poured out one piece of news after another in such rapid succession and without any regard as to order, that he heard good and bad, solemn and frivolous, all mixed together.

When they sailed down the inlet, a flag was hoisted over the canoe as a signal to the village that Duncan was on board. Soon he could see many flags flying over the village, and crowds of Indians hurrying to the landing beach. As he stepped out of the canoe a cannon went off, and then another, followed by a discharge of muskets from the corps of constables.

Then the formality broke. Everyone rushed at once to grab his hand, crowding and hemming him in so that he could hardly enter his house. Finally, his own emotions overcome, he stepped inside to compose himself, but the crowds so pressed in after him that he ordered the church bell rung. Everyone ran quickly, and by the time Duncan entered, the church was filled. He addressed the Indians for half an hour, then went to visit the sick and the aged who were anxiously begging to see him.

Back in his own house again, he soon found it filled with people, so he sat down with about fifty for a talk, telling them all about his trip. They sat and talked till midnight. When they finally left, the village was still wide awake, as the people were all waiting to hear from the favored fifty what had been said. Many did not go to bed at all that night but sat up excitedly talking over what they had heard.

Finally left alone in his house, Duncan could not help but reflect how different this was from the reception he had received from the same people when he had first arrived.

19

Metlakatla had made great strides ahead in the
1870's. Eagerly learning to use the wonderful new
equipment Duncan had brought back from England,
the Indians soon had the village humming with industry. There was the cooper's shop, the clog manufactur-
ing shop, the sash and door shop, and a brand-new
building for the weaving enterprise. No project
seemed too great in the new era of expansion.

The Indians even determined to rebuild their village in a more substantial manner. Gradually the
old dwellings were replaced with eighty-seven new
double houses of two-story height, provided with windows and chimneys and other civilized improvements.
The building lots were eventually fenced in and
planted with flowers in front and vegetables in back.
Construction was begun on a two-story schoolhouse
and the Mission House, which replaced Duncan's original log cabin.

Most ambitious of all were the plans for a magnificent new church. Land was cleared and drained, and

the great logs were rafted to the mill for the heavy framework. By Christmas of 1874 the new church with a seating capacity of over one thousand was dedicated. Although it cost over $12,000, it was erected entirely by voluntary contributions, partly from the Indians and partly from personal friends and admirers of Duncan. The balance was paid by the business shops of the village — not one dollar of its cost was borne by the Church Missionary Society in London.

During these busy times the brass band was practicing. Duncan had given out the thirty instruments and the basic instructions, and had sent thirty Indians out into the woods to practice. After a few hours they had returned, assuring him that they knew how to use them. Duncan was not so sure. He decided he would have the instruments returned to his office after each practice session. Later on he invited the music teacher to come up from Victoria and give them detailed instruction for three months.

There seemed to be no limit to Duncan's energy and

resourcefulness; thus there eventually was no end to the work he accumulated. Working day and night he could not keep up with all his varied duties: preacher, schoolmaster, doctor, magistrate, chief of police, mayor; general manager of the store, sawmill and other shops; designer and architect; bookkeeper and bandleader; and advisor and arbiter of every little trouble and dispute arising among over nine hundred people only recently removed from savagery. Even the vigorous Duncan was ready to admit it was too much for one man to handle. He agreed to have Mr. W. H. Collison come from England to take over the job of schoolmaster, while his wife managed a girls' dormitory and training school.

When the Collisons were established there, Duncan could more freely leave Metlakatla occasionally. Thus when he heard that the ancient land rights of all the Indians of British Columbia were being threatened by white land grabbers, he immediately set out for Ottawa, the capital of the new Dominion, far away across the vast prairie lands of Canada.

Duncan insisted that it was the duty of the Dominion Government to protect the Indians from this attack on their rights. He persuaded the Dominion officials that failure to do so might result in an Indian uprising, the consequences of which could only be contemplated with horror and fear.

This unfair legislation being considered in the province of British Columbia was thus halted because of his efforts — at least for a time.

His successful visit to Ottawa drew the attention of important government people upon Metlakatla. Lord Dufferin, then the Governor-General of the Dominion, came to the village in a warship to see for himself what the young Yorkshire missionary had accomplished in the northern wilderness. The next important visitor was Captain Prevost, now Admiral Prevost, who had never before seen Metlakatla. Duncan cordially introduced the admiral as the father of the mission. The admiral was so impressed by what he saw that he made the village a gift of a set of street lamps as a symbol of the light that Metlakatla was spreading throughout the darkness around it.

A brilliant beacon light on the desolate Northwest Coast was precisely what Metlakatla had become, sending its splendid rays in all directions up and down the winding channels of the Inside Passage. Even as far away as Sitka, Alaska, and at Fort Wrangell, Alaska, the Tlingits and the Chilkats were inspired by the light from Metlakatla. Elsewhere along the coast there was little hope for the natives' declining population and their disappearing ancient culture. Chief Toy-a-att, at Fort Wrangell, spoke out for all the Northwest Coast Indians in his sad appeal:

"My brothers and friends, I come before you today to talk a little, and I hope that you will listen to what I say, and not laugh at me because I am an Indian. I am getting old and have not many summers yet to live on this earth. I want to speak a little of the past history of the Sitka Indians and of our present wants. In ages past, before white men came among us, the Indians of Alaska were barbarous, with brutish instincts. Tribal wars were continual; bloodshed and murder of daily occurrence, and superstition controlled our whole movements and our hearts. The white man's God we knew not of. Nature showed to us that there was a first great cause; beyond that all was blank. Our God was created by us; that is, we selected animals and birds which we revered as gods.

"In the course of time a change came over the spirit of our dreams. We became aware of the fact that we were not the only beings in the shape of man that inhabited this earth. White men appeared before us on the surface of the great waters in large ships which we called canoes. Where they came from we knew not, but supposed that they dropped from the clouds. The ships' sails we took for wings, and concluded that, like the birds of the air, they could fly as well as swim. As time advanced, the white men who visited our country introduced among us everything that is produced by nature and the arts of man. They also told us of a God, a Superior Being, Who created all things, even us the Indians. They told us that this God was in the heavens above, and that all mankind were His children. These things were told to us but we could not understand them.

"At the present time we are not the same people that we were a hundred years ago. Association with the white man has created a change in our habits and customs. We have seen and heard of the wonderful works of the white man. His ingenuity and skill have produced steamships, railroads, telegraphs and thousands of other things. His mind is far-reaching; whatever he desires, he produces. Each day the white man becomes more perfect while the Indian is at a standstill. Why is this? Is it because the God you have told us of is a white God, and that you, being of His color, have been favored by Him? Why, brothers, look at our skin; we are dark, we are not of your color, hence you call us Indians. Is this the reason that we are ignorant; is this the cause of our not knowing our Creator?

"My brothers, a change is coming. We have seen and heard of the wonderful things of this world, and desire to understand what we see and what we hear. We desire light. We want our eyes to become open. We have been in the dark too long, and we appeal to you, my brothers, to help us. Look at Fort Simpson and at Metlakatla. See the Indians there. In years gone by they were the worst Indians on this coast, the most brutal, barbarous and bloodthirsty. They were our sworn enemies and were continually at war with us. How are they now? Instead of our enemies, they are our friends. They have become partially educated and civilized. They can understand what they see and what they hear; they can read and write and are learning to become Christians.

"These Indians are British Indians. We have been told that the British Government is a powerful one, and we have also been told that the American Government is a more powerful one. We have been told that the President of the United States has control over all the people, both whites and Indians. We have been told how he came to be our great chief. He purchased this country from Russia, and in purchasing it, he also purchased us. We had no choice or say in the change. The change has been made and we are content. All we ask is justice. We ask that we be civilized, Christianized and educated. Give us a chance, and we will show to the world that we can become peaceable citizens and good Christians."

There was no doubt about it: Metlakatla's influence was indeed casting a new light all along the Inside Passage. Full of confidence for the mission's continued spiritual progress, Duncan wrote in his journal: "The enemy is only permitted to annoy, but not to destroy us, only to make us stand more to our arms, and look more imploringly and continually to heaven."

Even as he wrote these words, however, a new enemy was massing its war cloud over Metlakatla, but Duncan could not see the storm warning — it came from too unexpected a source.

2 0

THE NEW CHURCH with its belfry tower silhouetted against the dark mountains was an impressive sight to passing ships in the inlet. Inside, it was even more beautiful with mellow cedar paneling and carved woodwork all lovingly created by native craftsmen whose ancient heritage was skill in the art of wood carving. It would have been the pride of any community. But there it was, in the middle of the wilderness, the largest church north of San Francisco; yet it had no ordained minister, and was of no particular denomination!

As Metlakatla grew, Duncan was repeatedly urged by the Church to become an ordained clergyman; in fact, the title of bishop was held out to him as the next step if he would do so. But Duncan consistently declined; as a humble, lay missionary, had not God already granted His blessing on his work?

Also, he feared that once he was ordained, the Church would next desire to have the Mission conform to the elaborate service and ritual of the Church of England. Although a member of the English Church himself, Duncan had persistently declared that his mission was not to glorify the Church; it was to lead the Indians to a pure life, not to teach them dogmas; to make Christians out of them, yes — but not, specifically, Episcopalians, or any other denomination.

These views were upheld by the Missionary Society as long as the Reverend Henry Venn was its General Secretary. He had fully approved of Duncan's methods and results, and the Society had written many glowing reports of his wonderful Metlakatla Mission.

But now Henry Venn was dead, and a more ritualistic spirit began to dominate the Society. They suggested that the Mission be immediately turned into an Episcopal Church with full administration of the Sacraments. Once again they urged Duncan to become ordained, and once more, he refused.

The Society apparently imagined the Indians to be advanced Christians, and thought the ritual of the Church would be safe and proper for them to follow. But Duncan knew many of them were still mere babes in religious comprehension. The keynote of his success had been simplicity. The Tsimshians had formerly connected magical powers with elaborate ceremonies. In his simple services, Duncan had never lured them by impressive vestments, altars or other churchly paraphernalia. And, as Duncan grew in wisdom, he only saw more clearly that the garments and Order of

Service — especially the Sacrament of the Last Supper — would only bewilder the Indians in their present stage of progress.

When the officers of the Society could see that there was no prospect of Duncan becoming ordained, they sent a young clergyman to Metlakatla. Duncan realized it would not be long before the Mission would become a full-fledged Episcopal Church. For such a step, he could only foresee disaster. Feeling his honesty of purpose was now at stake, he decided to leave his beloved Mission and seek a fresh start elsewhere. After the Reverend Hall arrived on August 6, 1877, Duncan quietly left for Victoria to think about his future plans. He mentioned nothing of this to the Metlakatla Indians. He spoke no farewells to them, fearing they would revolt against the Church and make things difficult for the new Reverend Hall.

He hadn't been long in Victoria, however, when rumors of strange happenings came down the coast from Metlakatla. The young clergyman, in his inexperience, had preached to the Indians from the text of Joel the Prophet: "Your sons and your daughters shall prophesy, your old men shall dream dreams, your young men shall see visions." In his youthful enthusiasm he had vividly impressed this scene upon them. The wild imagination of the Indian was aroused, and before long some of them heard voices and saw visions in the forest.

Duncan's friends in Victoria urged him to hurry back at once before all the results of his lifelong work were lost in a bog of religious fanaticism.

Duncan returned and soon had the Indians straightened out, and the ringleaders scolded. He told them they were no better than the medicine men of old days who loved to fool and trick the people.

One of the Indians answered, "You are mistaken, sir; we have had revelations."

"Revelations, fiddlesticks!" retorted Duncan. Then turning to the clergyman, he asked, "Mr. Hall, is this God's work?"

The young clergyman, without hesitation replied, "No, sir, I am sorry to say it is not."

A short time after this occurrence, Bishop Bompas visited Metlakatla. When he heard the story, he decided that it was no place for a novice, even if he were

147

an ordained clergyman, and he advised London that Duncan should take up his work as before. The Reverend Hall was assigned to the Indians at Fort Rupert. Although lacking in experience with Indians at that time, the Reverend Hall went on to give years of devoted and valuable service in the Northwest Coast mission field.

Bishop Bompas really had come to Metlakatla with instructions from London to turn the Mission into an Episcopal Church, and to introduce the Sacrament of the Last Supper. However, the wise old bishop advised both the Church and the Society that these Indians needed very careful guidance; that he deemed it precarious to initiate any changes at that time. Also, he did not want to risk destroying or undermining in any way the wonderful Christian spirit he had found thriving in Metlakatla. Bishop Bompas left Metlakatla just exactly as he had found it — and with his blessing.

This postponed any radical changes for two years. But in 1879 the northern portion of British Columbia was officially designated the "Diocese of Caledonia," in which there were, at the time, only three clergymen and one lay preacher. The Reverend William Ridley was consecrated bishop of this Diocese, and designating Metlakatla as the Episcopal Seat of his See, he arrived in the little Indian village on the first of November.

What a strange sight the regal bishop made in Metlakatla, parading about in his full Episcopal vestments and claiming the title and address of "My Lord." At first the bishop had nothing but kind words for everyone, assuring them in his first interpreted speech that he had not come to interfere with Mr. Duncan but would willingly work with him.

However, since he had not yet mastered the language, there was really little he could do. On Sundays he was obliged to sit in a pew like the rest of the congregation and listen to the Indians sing English hymns in the Tsimshian tongue. He could recognize the familiar intonations of the Litany and the Lord's Prayer, even when clothed in the strange language.

In closing, the congregation chorused, in the rhythm of an old Gregorian chant, a Psalm which Duncan had translated and arranged for them.

It wasn't long, however, before the bishop suggested some improvements in this simple service — a little more of the ritual. And in a few months he made it clear that he thought it was wrong to deprive the Indians of the Sacrament of the Last Supper. It was over this issue that the bishop and Duncan most bitterly opposed each other. Duncan was certain that he was better able to judge the minds of the Indians than the bishop or men in London who had never even seen them.

Duncan had given this subject a great deal of serious and anxious consideration. He had even discussed it with his most advanced natives. They had all agreed the weaker ones might depend upon the Sacrament as a magical charm. Over the years, Duncan had frankly expressed in his reports to the Society, his reasons for delaying the administration of the Sacrament, and he wrote them out once again for the bishop:

1. Not so long ago these Indians had at least assumed the appearance of cannibals. They have since been taught that these rites are an atrocious sin. Now when told they are to partake of the Body and Blood of Christ, can they be expected to distinguish between the symbol and the real substance?
2. There is the danger they might come to look upon the Sacrament as a charm which will be a passport to Heaven. Their former superstitious ideas could easily foster such a belief.
3. The British law forbids any man to give an Indian intoxicating liquor, and punishes him for doing so. Now the Church would give it to him, and it would not be wrong.
4. The Indians have a passion for liquor. There is a special danger in offering them even a sip of wine in the Sacrament.
5. The law treats the Indians as children. It forbids the Indians from drinking liquors and punishes them for doing so. Certainly the Christian Church has never intended that children should partake of this Sacrament.

The bishop could see that against a man of Duncan's firmness he could get nowhere. He decided to bide his time. But his overbearing tactics soon provoked even the Reverend Hall at Fort Rupert and the Reverend Tomlinson at the Kincolith Mission on the Nass River. The Reverend Tomlinson, after refusing to carry out one of the bishop's orders, had returned to England and laid the matter before the Society.

The Society's officials began to realize they had created a most awkward situation in the North Pacific. Things were not going well in the new Diocese. Hoping to avoid further complications, they decided the missionary staff of the Diocese should meet annually in conference to settle their mission affairs. This little group at the first Conference, in 1881, comprised the following people: the Reverend Hall from Fort Rupert; the Reverend Tomlinson, who since 1867 had successfully headed a mission up the Nass River; the Reverend Collison, the former schoolmaster; Bishop Ridley; William Duncan; and the two present schoolmasters, Mr. Schutt and Mr. Chantrel.

After matters concerning the other mission stations had been settled, they took up the problems of Metlakatla. The bishop stayed away from this part of the Conference.

Feeling that a crisis had now arrived, Duncan determined to place the entire responsibility of the dilemma upon the Conference, and to stand by their decision. He reminded them he was only a layman, and the Society now preferred an ordained man in charge of the Mission. In view of this he asked the Conference whether they would advise him to resign his connection with Metlakatla. They unanimously declined to advise him to resign.

This gave rise to another problem. After all these years it would be awkward and confusing for the Indians to have anyone else supersede Duncan. How was the difficulty involved in his staying to be met? Duncan asked the Conference if they would consent to advise the Society to allow Metlakatla to assume its complete independence — to work out its own destiny and bear all of its own expenses.

The Conference resolved to ask the Society to consider turning Metlakatla into an Independent Mission. Their request, along with a full report, was sent off to London on the next steamer. After receiving the Conference's report, the Society wrote a letter to Duncan inviting him — not summoning him, but *inviting* him — to come to London to confer with them on the future status of Metlakatla.

This letter, dated September 29, 1881, was received by Duncan while he was in Victoria purchasing machinery for a salmon cannery. He answered the invitation, stating that he could not leave right away, as it would mean postponing the installation of this important new industry for another year. As soon as the machinery was installed, however, he would immediately leave for England.

The steamer that brought Duncan back to Metlakatla from Victoria, having to unload all the cannery machinery, was delayed in the harbor an extra day.

Duncan had barely turned the key in his own door when the bishop rushed in, asking, "Are you going back to England to meet the Society?"

"Not at the present time," was Duncan's reply.

The bishop then thrust a letter into Duncan's hand. It was from London.

> Salisbury Square
> London, E. C.,
> September 29, 1881
>
> To Mr. W. Duncan
>
> Dear Brother Duncan:
>
> The envelope containing this letter is placed in the hands of the bishop with a request that he will hand it to you *only* in the event of your refusing to come home to confer with the committee, and continuing your opposition to the spiritual work of the mission being carried on in accord with the principles of the Church of England as accepted by this Society.
>
> With the deepest pain and sorrow the committee has come to the conclusion, that in such a contingency they have no course to pursue, but to take the necessary steps for dissolving your connection with the Society. . . .

This letter was also dated September 29, 1881 — the same date as the one Duncan had received in Victoria. But this letter had been sent as an enclosure directly to the bishop, who had been instructed to deliver it to Duncan *only* in case Duncan refused to go to England. The bishop knew from Duncan's own lips that he had not refused, but in his impatience to get rid of Duncan, he had overstepped his authority and handed him the fateful letter.

Meanwhile, the Society had received Duncan's letter telling them he would come home after the cannery machinery was installed. The Society knew this was not a refusal and immediately wrote to the bishop instructing him not to give Duncan that letter. But it was too late. The bishop had already done so, and was himself on the way to London. Fearful of his own hasty action, and thinking he had better explain himself in person, the bishop had immediately fled to England on the same steamer that had just brought Duncan back.

As soon as the Metlakatlans became aware of what had happened, they called their own meeting. After several strong speeches were presented, one of the elders of the church put the question to them, "Will you have the bishop or Shimauget for your leader?"

"Shimauget!" shook the solid cedar walls.

Duncan was sent for. George Usher, one of the Indian elders, approached him, Bible in hand, and turning to the congregation, said, "You are now asked to confirm with your own voices whether you wish Mr. Duncan to continue as your teacher and minister. All of you who so desire, show it now to Mr. Duncan by holding out your hand to him."

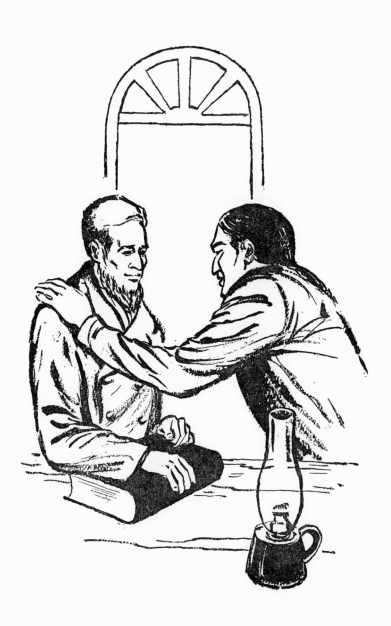

Every hand in the audience went out to their beloved teacher. Every voice spoke his name.

The elder turned to Duncan, placed the Bible in his hand and said: "In behalf of this Christian congregation, I say to you: continue to be our minister, and go on teaching the Word of God, as you have done for the last twenty-four years."

It was the only ordination as a minister that Duncan ever had. Now he knew for certain that he could never leave them. He had faced all the past terrors and loneliness, stood uncompromisingly against medicine men, chiefs and whiskey traders, and he would not be found wanting now. He would stay and protect them from any calamity. He was no longer a Yorkshire Englishman; he was one of them — a Metlakatlan.

21

THE HARMONY of Metlakatla was hopelessly shattered. Even in faraway London there was discord. The Society's office was in a turmoil. Bishop Ridley had returned but his explanation met only with disapproval. It looked as if the Society's efforts to bring Metlakatla in line with church policy had instead caused the loss of their most spectacular foreign mission. The Metlakatla Indians were now, by their own unanimous vote, "Duncan's Indians," not the Society's Indians. There was no longer one single solitary soul in Metlakatla to whose spiritual needs the bishop could have an opportunity to administer.

In desperation the Society sent the bishop back to the Northwest with orders to move heaven and earth to persuade Duncan and all the Indians to return to the fold.

Duncan's only answer was, "Too late." He vacated the Mission House and the schoolhouse, the only buildings erected with the help of the Society's funds, and handed over the keys and records to the bishop.

The bishop promptly moved in and managed to lure to his side a few disgruntled former chiefs and two native schoolteachers. After four or five months there really was, then, a "bishop's party" at Metlakatla, consisting of five or six people. With this small foothold gained for the Society, the bishop began to undermine Duncan and the Independent Mission.

It was the beginning of five years of tension and intrigue. The bishop's first maneuver was an attempt to destroy the economy of the Metlakatlans. Their most reliable source of income was from the successful village store. Obtaining supplies with Society funds, the bishop opened a competitive store in the Mission House, and began to sell at cost prices. Although the Metlakatlans refused to trade with him, Indians from outside were tempted by the lower prices, and his scheme at least partially succeeded.

But it was not successful enough to crush them into submission. He then asserted that the original village store belonged to the Society, although none of the Society's funds had ever been used either to build it or stock it. The Society had never assumed any connection with the village store; nor had they ever asked to see any accounting of its profits over the years. The Society's only financial aid to the Mission had been help with the building of the Mission House and the schoolhouse plus the small salary paid to Duncan as a missionary and teacher.

That Duncan had added to these labors was not by their orders, nor at their cost or risk — it was not even for their benefit. They had approved and acclaimed his success, but the economic success of the village had been at his own cost, his own risk, and for the sole benefit of the Indians. The village store, the workshops, the church and all the public improvements had been built and operated through their own resourcefulness — their profits from their industries plus the donations of interested friends.

Since the original village store was uncomfortably close to the Mission House, the Indians sought legal advice, and, acting upon that advice, proceeded to take down the store and move it to a new, less irritating location.

Although this was done in an orderly fashion, the bishop read the riot act, sending such an alarming report to Victoria that the authorities immediately sent a warship to the scene.

In fact, not having a British warship in the vicinity at that time and not daring to wait, they prevailed upon the United States government to send up the revenue cutter *Oliver Wolcott*.

However, the two magistrates aboard could find no signs of riot in Metlakatla and dismissed the case.

It was the first of many incidents which invariably ended with the bishop calling for another warship. These skirmishes were of no great significance to the Indians outside of Metlakatla.

But now the bishop asserted a claim which alarmed the entire native population of British Columbia. The bishop now proclaimed that the two acres of land on which the Mission buildings stood belonged to the Society. Most frightening of all, he also stated that the government of British Columbia supported this claim.

This unjust claim upon the ancient heritage of the Indians was in direct contradiction to the principle recognized by England throughout the rest of Canada in dealing with Indians' land rights: the Indians have the right of possession which can only be taken from them by conquest, or obtained through treaty and compensation. Under Lord Dufferin as Governor-General of Canada this pledge had been faithfully kept. But the pledge of Lord Dufferin went unheeded in the province of British Columbia.

In the early years when the Hudson's Bay Company ruled the land, and later, as a Crown Colony under the leadership of Governor Douglas, the Indians' right to title of the land had been strictly upheld, but the wise and dominating influence of Sir Douglas, who died in 1877, was over.

For the next decade political conditions in the province steadily declined as corrupt officials and land grabbers manipulated legislation for their own gain. By 1886 the authorities in office were openly proclaiming that the Indians had no rights in the lands which they and their ancestors had possessed for centuries before the coming of the white man; and that they were wholly dependent on the grace and bounty of the Crown for permission to occupy any lands at all.

By virtue of this alleged title and ownership of the

land, the bishop now turned traitor to the interests of all the Indians of the province by demanding that the government survey and set aside to the Missionary Society the two acres in question.

The Indians were enraged and confused; whom were they to believe? Were they to throw aside their long-treasured trust in the justice of British law? It was all Duncan could do to maintain calm and reason among them. Assuring them that the Dominion government would never allow this to happen, he left immediately for Ottawa.

The Premier listened with sympathetic interest to Duncan's plea for the Indians' rights. He asked Duncan to present in writing a plan for the relief of the Indians' problems. This he did.

The plan involved the appointment of a local Superintendent of Indian Affairs, whose orders, however, would originate in Ottawa, not in British Columbia.

The Premier approved the plan and promised to carry it through at the next session of the Dominion Parliament. He also promised to prevail upon the Society to withdraw entirely from Metlakatla.

"There is one difficulty," said the Premier as Duncan rose to leave. "Unless we could secure the services of yourself as superintendent, I would despair of its success."

"Very well," replied Duncan, "to help the Indians out, I will consent to act as superintendent for one year, on condition that I receive no salary."

"Good," answered the Premier, "that settles it. In six months your proposed plan shall be the law of the land."

With this hopeful news the Indian delegates accompanying Duncan returned home, but Duncan decided his wisest move was to return to England until the plans were legally resolved. He knew the mission was in good hands for his friends had rallied around him: the Reverend Tomlinson, having previously resigned from the Society's service, had come to Metlakatla to become Duncan's most trusted friend and co-worker — a graduate of Dublin University, he was a physician as well as a clergyman; Dr. Bluett-Duncan, a British physician on a vacation tour of the province, had remained to offer his services; and Sir Henry Wellcome, a wealthy Englishman who, having become a devoted admirer of Duncan's work, had felt compelled to write a book about the Mission which he published at his own expense.

Nor had his friends in Victoria forgotten him or remained silent; the Victoria *Daily Colonist* was filled with indignant letters and editorials.

Back in England Duncan waited the stipulated six months. He heard nothing. After waiting two more months, he returned by way of Ottawa where he sought an interview with the Premier but could not get it. He wrote to the Deputy Minister of Indian Affairs who promised to have an answer for him in Metlakatla. Then he continued on to the Mission to await further news.

No answer, no acknowledgement ever came. It eventually became evident that there had been an unabashed shift in policy; that the promises made at Ottawa were empty promises and had been violated for political reasons.

Instead, a government surveying party, sent out by the Dominion government, arrived in Metlakatla in the fall of 1886. Although there had been no answer to the Indians' appeal for help, although no treaty had ever been made with them for the land they were now being called upon to surrender, the government began to survey the land it intended to take away from the Indians.

The Metlakatlans were desperate. They knew a government survey was no answer to all their appeals for help. It was only the beginning of the end.

The time had come when their ancient title to the land must be decided once and forever in a court of law. There was no longer any alternative except to force a test case into the court. This they accomplished by erecting a small, temporary building on the two acres of land which the government was saying belonged to the Society.

The time had also come to demonstrate their protest. Without resorting to violence they did this by preventing the survey from being made. When a surveyor planted his instrument, an Indian quietly took it up. When the surveyor drove a stake, an Indian pulled it up. When the surveyors laid a chain, the Indians calmly took it away.

163

The outcome of this protest was the usual one — the warship *Cormorant* was dispatched to Metlakatla to enforce the survey, and seven Tsimshians were arrested, hauled aboard the warship and taken to Victoria to be jailed.

Indians all along the Northwest Coast viewed the situation in Metlakatla with alarm and exasperation. Fear of an Indian war mounted among the white settlers, and the letters and editorials grew more indignant than ever.

Duncan's old friend, the Reverend Cridge, now Bishop Cridge, also spoke out in the newspapers. Bishop Cridge, the first resident clergyman on the Northwest Coast, had the following remarks to make in the Victoria *Daily Colonist* on October 28, 1886:

. . . The dispatch of another warship against the Metlakatlans leads me to solicit a space in your columns for a few words in the interests of justice and peace. . . . The Metlakatlans have been guilty of no illegal acts, nor hostile demonstrations in the steps they have taken to establish their rights to their ancient inheritance. . . . The Society who were permitted to occupy the site of the Mission House solely on account of services rendered to the inhabitants, now that those services are no longer required, still hold possession, apparently claiming ownership or at least the right of perpetual occupancy. The Metlakatlans, therefore, have taken, without violence or riot, the step of erecting a building on the land in question with the sole view of bringing this contention to a legal issue. They are prepared to abide by the ultimate decision of the law, whatever that may be. . . . The tribes far and near are watching the case with intense anxiety, as that on which their own rights depend. They will regard forcible seizure at Metlakatla as the forerunner of what will happen to themselves, and there are not wanting signs to show that in such a case they will be exasperated and alarmed in the highest degree. If war ensues, these down-trodden members of the human family must be conquered in the end, but the whole guilt of innocent blood will surely rest on those who rejected the peaceable means of settlement provided by the law and instead sought it by force. Your obedient servant, Edward Cridge, Bishop R.E.C., Resident since 1854.

Tension mounted all along the coastline as the Indians awaited a court decision on Metlakatla. For the first time in its history no British flag was raised over Metlakatla. The cry of the Thunderbird returned to the land; the war clouds hovered low over all British Columbia, and no one dared predict what the outcome might be.

22

Duncan journeyed to Victoria to await the court's decision on Metlakatla. Here he could at least pass the trying days of waiting by sightseeing and visiting with his old friends. Once before he had marked time in Victoria. Recalling those first months in the Northwest awaiting permission to go on to Fort Simpson, he concluded that the passing years had not made him one whit more adaptable to waiting. Was it really twenty-nine years ago?

Duncan was present in court when the chief justice announced from the bench his decision granting the bishop's claim to the two acres. So the ugly words were finally out and officially spoken — that the Indians had no rights in the land except such as might be accorded to them by the bounty and charity of the Queen of England. Duncan immediately dispatched the exact words of the justice to the Reverend Tomlinson in Metlakatla. As soon as it was received, the Native Council called a meeting.

Duncan knew nothing of this decisive meeting until

two weeks later when a group of Metlakatlans arrived in Victoria to see him. Acting suspicious of everyone, the Indians insisted they could not tell him their important news except in secrecy. Duncan arranged to meet with them the following day at the home of a close friend.

Meanwhile, Duncan went to see the Provincial Secretary, Mr. Robson, the only member of the local government who seemed to have any sympathy for the Indians. When they were settled alone in the study, Duncan told him, "A delegation of Indians has just arrived from the North to see me. They are reticent and will not tell me their errand. I am afraid that this bodes no good. I come to you now, for the last time, to see if anything can be done to stop this trouble. I can speak now, for I know nothing. Tomorrow, after I have seen them and know what they have concluded to do, my mouth will probably be sealed, so I can tell you nothing. Their decision, as far as I can imagine, can be the result of only two possible choices. One is to leave for Alaska. If it be that, all is well and good. If you hear tomorrow night that I have left for the States, you may know that it is Alaska. But, if I do not leave, I am afraid that it means fight. And if it does, may God have mercy on the white people of this province. You will need to send five thousand men up there. And they will go there only to be killed: the Indians will withdraw up the Skeena River, and all the military you can send will be simply slaughtered in the canyons, while the Indians will go comparatively free.

Your treasury will be depleted. Your population will be murdered. Your soldiers will be slaughtered. But if it is 'fight,' don't come to me anymore. Don't try to get me to do anything. For I will not. I am going to leave you all to your fate now. I have pleaded and preached and prayed till I am sick at heart at the injustice you have showered on those poor Indians."

The next day in privacy the Indians eagerly re-counted the details of the Council meeting to Duncan. The Council had met in a mood of desperation. Their plight seemed hopeless. The troubles of the past years had drained their finances. The money spent on the Ottawa trip was wasted; certainly there were no funds left to send another delegation all the way to England to seek help directly from Queen Victoria, and even if they could, they feared that long chance could only end in a bog of red tape. No matter where they ap-pealed they encountered such overwhelming opposi-tion — from the ministers of state, the church, the courts — that they despaired of ever finding justice in their own country.

Some of the Indians were for fighting openly. "We might as well make a last stand; as well fight, kill and die as let these robbers take away from us the land our forefathers possessed for hundreds of years before a white man set foot in British Columbia." Others agreed. They had reached the limit of their endur-ance; there was nothing else left to live for. "There is no longer any virtue in enduring this oppression and intolerance. To fight would be more valiant."

But the war cries lacked fervor. Once the Tsimshians were powerful and daring in war, but civilization had shorn them of their barbaric strength and capacity for warfare. Once they would have met any invasion of their rights with a swift and savage attack, but the cry of the Thunderbird and the beat of the medicine drum no longer stirred their blood. No longer did their warriers thirst for blood and the spoils of the warpath; no longer did their heroes return to dance and chant the ancient legends. It was only a memory now. Gone forever were the mystical powers of Raven, Eagle, Wolf and Bear. Those braves of other days, in yielding to civilization and the pursuit of knowledge had surrendered themselves to the mercy of the white man. Even the Indians most avid to fight knew that this was really so.

The more earnest Christians among them had another plan in mind: an idea that had been talked about for some time. They finally subdued the others into listening to them.

"A Christian can suffer. He can die. But he cannot kill," they said. "Let us go to the great land of the free. We are slaves here. There we can be free men. We love this land. We love this beautiful place where our fathers lived, and where our children were born; but we love God more. Two wrongs cannot make one right. Let us go to Alaska where we can worship God as we think right — where there will be no bishop to worry and tantalize us — where, as Mr. Duncan tells us, everyone can have his own religion without any

170

persecution, either from church or government. Let us go to this peaceful life; let us go to Alaska!"

Thus having told Duncan of the Council's final decision, they all began to ask questions of him at once: Did he really believe the United States would let them move to Alaska? Would he represent them? Would he go to Washington and seek permission? Would they be received as citizens and protected in their rights? Would they be able to take down their houses and bring their possessions with them? Did he really think they could do it?

For the first time in many months Duncan felt a surge of his former optimism, and a great feeling of hope and excitement filled his heart. Of course he would go, and he would not waste another minute; he would leave immediately for Washington, D.C. He would go straight to the President of the United States.

23

Wɪᴛʜ ʜɪs ᴄᴜsᴛᴏᴍᴀʀʏ ᴛʜᴏʀᴏᴜɢʜɴᴇss Duncan arrived in Washington well armed with impressive introductions from Governor Swineford of the Territory of Alaska, Sheldon Jackson, U.S. General Agent of Education, and William H. Dall, scientific explorer in the North Pacific.

From Victoria he had a letter signed by Bishop Cridge and other friends of influence there. And he had not appealed in vain to men like Episcopalian Bishop Phillips Brooks in Boston, and Henry Ward Beecher in Brooklyn. Both of them had opened their magnificent churches to him, and in a unanimous written request by their congregations, had asked the government to grant the Indians a refuge in Alaska. These letters took him exactly where he wanted to go — straight to President Cleveland.

On January 6, 1887 the President arranged for Duncan to speak before the Board of Indian Commissioners. Eloquently and convincingly, Duncan spoke on behalf of his beloved Indians. At subsequent sessions the government officials were able to question Duncan about the Indians' problems in Metlakatla. It wasn't long before Duncan was assured that the Indians were welcome to choose a homesite for themselves in southeastern Alaska. Although nothing official could be done immediately which might be construed by Great Britain as an unfriendly act toward Canada, the officials promised that, in time, action would be taken by Congress to secure their rights. This promise was fulfilled by Congress in the Act of March 3, 1891.

Duncan immediately dispatched the good news to the Reverend Tomlinson and Dr. Bluett-Duncan, suggesting that a group of Indians should leave at once to examine various eligible sites for the new home.

Five Indians, accompanied by Dr. Bluett-Duncan, set out on a voyage of exploration. Entering the open waters of Dixon Entrance, they crossed the boundary line between British Columbia and Alaska, headed north into Clarence Strait and then into Nichols Passage. Seventy miles north of the old village they came to a beautiful bay on the northwest side of Annette Island. Rounding a headland, the six explorers stopped paddling and silently viewed the scene before them.

A curiously shaped little island lay across the entrance of the bay like a ship at anchor. A graceful sweep of dark sand edged the water, and behind this splendid canoe beach the sloping forest merged into a distinctly purple mountain, rising two thousand five hundred feet above the sea. Even at their distance from it, they could hear the noisy splashing of a hidden

waterfall cascading down the mountainside. Above
the green forest, the jagged snowcapped ranges min-
gled with long strips of gray clouds.

Silently enjoying the beauty before them, the explorers drifted along with the current. It was a day
created for good omens, and unexpectedly, the Indians
had one: a great voice suddenly arose, swelling and
rolling over the land until it filled the air with magnificent, musical trumpeting. It was the powerful voice of
the trumpeter swan, who lived by the lake in the valley
of the purple mountain.

Finally, as the sonorous voice died away, one of the
Indians spoke. "It is no use to go any farther. . . .

We can certainly not find anything finer than this if we go a thousand miles."

The others were equally impressed, and thus on March 25, 1887, Annette Island, in southeastern Alaska, was selected as the Metlakatlans' new home.

The explorers eagerly returned home to give a glowing account of their discovery: the fine beach for landing canoes; the forests for timber; the fresh water stream and the great waterfall for water power; plus the peaceful beauty of the sheltered bay. Their selection was soon ratified by the Indian Council.

Duncan, still in the States, was notified, and a party of Indians set out for Annette Island to build temporary huts while the rest of the Indians remained at Metlakatla for the usual season of fishing and preserving the winter's supply of food.

By August another party of men, having returned from the fishing camps, set out in their canoes for Alaska. Later, Duncan, too, arrived at Annette Island. He was accompanied by several American friends who carried with them a brand new American flag. A temporary flagstaff was rigged up, and the Stars and Stripes waved for the first time on Annette Island.

Duncan supervised the unloading of a complete steam sawmill outfit purchased in Portland, Oregon. Since it filled to overflowing the little log house built for him to live in, he was obliged to camp out in a tent until the sawmill was erected.

George Usher was sent back to old Metlakatla with the news that Duncan had arrived and had officially dedicated the new home. As the Indian skimmed over the waters of the North Pacific, he composed a chant for his people. Upon arrival, instead of running his canoe up onto the beach, he stopped, Indian-style, a little distance from the shore. When all the people had seen him there, and were gathered together along the beach, he began his chant in the Tsimshian tongue:

> The great chief has come,
> He has gone to our new home.
> Now he sends me to you,
> He bids you come, one and all.
> We shall be slaves no longer.
> The land of freedom has accepted us,
> The flag of the "Boston men" * is hoisted
> At the site of a new Metlakatla.

* Term used to signify Yankees, or Americans in general, since Clipper ship days when most American ships had sailed out of Boston.

It will protect us and our freedom,
We can worship God in peace.
We can secure the happiness of our children.
They will be the freemen of a great nation.
Come, therefore, one and all,
Gather your little ones around you,
Push the canoes from the beach.
Good wind will fill our sails;
We will hasten to the land of freedom.

The last note had barely died away when ten canoes filled with men eager to see their new home with their own eyes were on their way to Alaska.

After additional huts were built, the pioneers returned for their families and all their possessions.

Duncan had previously written to the Secretary of the Treasury of the United States inquiring whether the Indians could transport their goods duty free, and

the reply had been yes. For this reason a cannery steamer was standing by ready to be loaded.

But it was not to be. Even at the last moment ugly persecution again asserted itself, and they were denied the right to take along even the windows and doors of the houses they had built, the sawmill machinery, the looms, lathes and other machinery they owned and had paid for. Even the church organ, to which every Indian had contributed his $2.50, was denied them.

In spite of this heavy loss, eight hundred and twenty-three resolute Indians turned their canoe prows toward the North, and empty-handed sailed forth to a strange new land. More important than their ancestral homeland, more important than all their material possessions, was their great hope for a bright new future in Alaska.

24

WILLIAM DUNCAN was fifty-five years old that first year in new Metlakatla, but he looked years younger. Behind his enthusiasm and the sparkle in his blue eyes there was another, more elusive quality in his personality, the result of his many years in the wilderness. He had learned to tread the dark rain forests as silently as his Indian comrades, and he had been enriched by his close contact with nature.

Shortly after their arrival in Alaska, Duncan assembled all the men together to explain their responsibilities to their adopted country. Gathered around their leader, all those dark-eyed men, young and old, held up their right hands and solemnly swore allegiance to the United States. It was not a legal proceeding for they were not yet citizens, but Duncan knew the effect on the Indians would be the same as if it had been official. He wanted to bind them at once with the ties of allegiance to their new country.

He did not, however, want anyone to feel bound to the new village because of having built an expensive house. Consequently, for the first two years everyone lived in temporary huts built among stumps and trees, both standing and fallen. The dense forest extended down to the beach, and before an orderly village could take shape, the giant trees had to be felled and the stumps hauled away. Also, of more importance to the Indians than sturdy homes were the public buildings they needed right away: a steam sawmill and village store, a lumber shed which doubled as a church and a shelter for the school.

Since the first school shelter had no fireplace, Duncan and his three native assistants often called recess so the children could warm themselves by a scamper on the beach. The girls played tag, and the boys rushed to their favorite game of marbles. Duncan observed that an Indian boy was as proud of his bag of marbles as any white boy, and several times he found them playing marbles after school in the pouring rain, or by lantern light on a dark winter afternoon.

In teaching the children to read and write in English, Duncan felt hampered by the lessons furnished in the primary reading books, which he thought had too much nonsense about cats owning tails and dogs being able to bark. To the Indian child eager to learn new things, all such information appeared very ridiculous when translated into his mother tongue.

During one recess period Duncan took the children to watch a particularly huge spruce tree being cut down. The great tree was cut about twenty-four feet

from the ground and made to fall in a certain direction to avoid crushing nearby buildings. The men were so elated with their success that they nailed a pole on top with four small American flags attached to it, and all the excited children gave a loud cheer. This high stump became the base for an elevated bandstand from which the brass band played concerts for visiting friends and government officials.

It was hard work, creating a village out of the wilderness of Annette Island, and Duncan's unlimited capacity for all kinds of work was fully used in those first years in Alaska.

Steady progress was being made until the day the sawmill caught fire. A dry gale from the north had been blowing for several weeks, and everything was tinder dry. Before they were able to halt the blaze, the mill and all their sawed and dressed lumber burned to the ground. They had arrived in Alaska practically penniless; now they were in serious financial trouble.

Duncan took the next mail steamer to Portland, Oregon, and by obtaining extended time payments, managed to purchase machinery for a new sawmill. When the Mission's many friends heard of the fire, they came to their rescue with generous donations of money, and progress once again got under way.

Before long a salmon cannery was completed, but there was no money to operate this industry on the scale necessary to make it profitable. After carefully thinking it over, Duncan decided to ask his friends for help. He formed a corporation called "The Metlakatla Industrial Company," and friends were asked to buy shares in it, with the understanding that if the enterprise succeeded, they would be repaid the money advanced. If not, they would lose it, and neither Duncan nor the Indians would be under obligation to repay them.

Early in spring before the salmon run started, Indian workers began making tin cans and wooden crates. During the summer as the fishermen brought in the catch, the salmon were processed — cut, cleaned and packed into cans. As in the primitive days — when everyone worked during a run — there was a job for anyone who wanted it in the salmon cannery: the women packed the fish by hand, their sensitive fingers carefully discarding any pieces of sick salmon; the girls wiped off the cans, and the boys stacked them. After the lids were soldered on, the cans were put in the boiler for the first cooking. Then a hole was punched in each can to allow air to escape, again soldered, and the cans replaced in the boiler for their second cooking.

After being carefully tested for leaks, the cans were set aside until the season was over when they were tested again — then lacquered, labelled and marketed. Under Duncan's constant supervision, the cannery workers and all the equipment were kept scrupulously clean. Near the end of the season the salmon were apt to become flabby. As soon as Duncan noticed the fish losing their prime condition, he immediately closed down, and not another fish was allowed to be canned.

The new cannery was a success: the Indians were paid fair wages and the stockholders were repaid their money with interest. All the industries did well — the store, sawmill and lumber shops — and eventually Duncan was able to set aside a trust fund for the Mission, thus securing its financial future.

Meanwhile, private dwellings had begun to take permanent architectural form; mostly square, two-story houses with wide porches. A queer looking structure with twelve gables, first used as the church, became the Town Hall. The strange, octagonal design of

some of the buildings was created to better resist the violent windstorms which swept over Annette Island during the winter months. Because the warm Japanese Current flowed through Alaskan waters, snow was a novelty on the island except on the mountaintops, and the temperature rarely fell below freezing.

For several years the Indians had also been working on their most spectacular project, a magnificent new church. By Christmas Day of 1896 it was ready to be dedicated. With the entire village crowded into its fragrant, cedar-paneled sanctuary, the Indians raised their voices in songs of praise. Harmonious fragments of sound — from the chanting voices, the pipe organ and the pealing church bell — were wafted away on

gusts of wind to blend with all the mysterious music of the sea and forest. For these musical people the voice of the trumpeter swan had indeed been a symbolic omen.

The largest church in all Alaska, it became known throughout the territory as "Mr. Duncan's Westminster Abbey." Its twin white towers rose eighty feet above the ground, reaching skyward against the dramatic background of Purple Mountain. But its name and creed were direct and simple: "The Christian Church of Metlakatla" it was called, and it was not affiliated with any denomination.

In their present stage of understanding, Duncan at last felt the Indians were ready to receive the Sacrament of the Last Supper. With no rituals imposed, it was inaugurated as a simple communion service, held about three times a year.

True to the convictions of his youth, Duncan said of the Alaska Mission, "I have kept out all sects and denominational rule. We are simply 'Christians,' nothing else, at Metlakatla. The Word of God has united us, not split us up into parties, and we love and treat all men as our brothers."

As the years sped by, Duncan seldom left the island. He would have been welcomed as a lecturer in the United States, but he always found something that needed his attention at home. Schoolteachers and physicians came and went, devoting a year or two of their careers to the Mission, but in between he still found himself in charge of everything.

Neighboring Tlingit Indians, knowing that they would be fairly dealt with, paddled to Metlakatla to have their disputes settled by Commissioner Duncan. There was rarely any trouble among the Metlakatlans, but sometimes echoes of the ancient potlatch practice cropped up, and he found it necessary to settle disputes over gifts and debts which had become ridiculously complicated.

Sometimes he thought he might take a trip "outside" after the salmon season was over. But how could he leave then? He might not get back in time for Christmas . . . and Christmas in Metlakatla, with all its joy and music, was a time he would not miss. Haidas and Tlingits were drawn to the village then, and it was not unusual to see the canoes of many visitors pulled up on the beach during the holidays.

Before he knew it, the canning season had come again, and by midsummer his friends were arriving in Alaska to visit him, so he certainly could not leave then.

All kinds of music flourished on the island. When the brass band went on tour to Pacific Coast cities, there was still plenty of music left at home: the reed band; the string band; the orchestra; the girls' zobo band; several pianos and forty-six organs. In October of 1907 everyone who so desired had his chance to play at the Fiftieth Anniversary celebration of Duncan's arrival at Fort Simpson.

Now at age seventy-five, Duncan's hair was white

and he had a full white beard, but these were the only clues to his advanced age, for his erect carriage, ruddy cheeks and vitality bespoke a much younger man. The Indians presented him with a leather armchair, and many speeches were made. There were several among them who had been at Fort Simpson so long ago, and Duncan fondly recalled others, such as Paul Legaic, and his first friend and interpreter, Clah, who had died before coming to the new Metlakatla.

Knowing his fondness for music, the choir (with organ) had prepared a special performance of Handel's "Messiah" for him. As he listened to the crescending tones, the echos of their earlier music came to his mind — the simple strains of a young man's accordion, accompanied by the primitive rhythms of rattles and drums.

One flaw marred Duncan's thankfulness in that anniversary year: the Tsimshians had not yet been granted U.S. citizenship. Nevertheless, they were far better off than the rest of the Alaskan natives, that Duncan knew. As more people migrated to Alaska following the gold rush at the turn of the century, the natives — both Indians and Eskimos — began to lose their mastery over a difficult land.

The Northwest Coast Indian had always depended mainly upon the sea for his living. There was no other place he could go and still carry on his own way of life. He had two choices: he could either go to work for the white man or he could try to compete with him as an independent fisherman. Neither choice benefited him.

As the Indian's old customs crumbled away, he tried to copy the white man's pattern of life. But in this attempt he swayed uncertainly. Lacking in experience, as Duncan had recognized so long ago, the Indian was not able to make a happy transition from ancient to modern ways. Bearing out the doom predicted by the Tsimshian chiefs of old, the population along the coast sadly dwindled.

The Alaska natives desperately wanted schools; they waited patiently for the education and protection which would have halted the trend of disease and guided them wisely into the civilized world. Concerned Alaskans spoke out for the natives, but government help was slow in coming. Until 1912 Alaska had no official territorial status, and even that was so limited in scope, the residents still had little to say about their own destiny. Their affairs were largely controlled by powerful "outside" companies that financed the rich mining and fishing industries. Like the sea traders of old, their interest was only in taking profits out of Alaska; not in the welfare of the people. Against their influence, Alaska's handful of residents were no match, and with no official voice in Washington, their pleas for the neglected natives went unheard.

Symbolic of the natives' plight were the toppled totem poles to be found rotting away all over southeastern Alaska. Only in Metlakatla was there something of value to replace the once great powers of

Raven, Eagle, Wolf and Bear. As Duncan had hoped, sailing down the Nass River so many years ago, the Metlakatlans had eternal values to sustain them in any crisis.

As he entered his eighties, visitors sometimes asked him, "What have you done about appointing someone to take your place here?" But Duncan, who in all other matters had always shown concern for every detail, simply shook his head from side to side, and pointed a finger to the heavens. His heart rested in confidence that the Indians could manage their future alone; if it were not so, of what use had been his lifetime spent among them? He felt no need to comment on this question. It was enough now just to enjoy every moment of every day on the beautiful North Pacific island, the joy of sharing the radiant flowering of summer with friends and tourists, in listening to the glorious music that filled the church, in watching the happy children, whose round, dark-eyed faces looked so exactly like those other children of years ago.

How fast the seasons seemed to come and go . . . how quickly the autumn mists were followed by the winter winds howling outside his cozy fireplace. But content with his clutter of books and letters, he welcomed the solitude to which he was accustomed. Recollections flooded his mind; he would not have traded places with anyone else on earth. He died peacefully at home in 1918. In his memory, the Indians erected a monument carved with a hand holding a torch. They

chose this symbol because, as they said, "he brought us the Light."

As Duncan had known they would, the Metlakatlans moved steadily forward into the first half of the twentieth century. Following Pearl Harbor, air power came to Annette Island. Until the United States established a base on the island, there had been no airfield in Southeastern Alaska. Except for small sea planes, transportation had been entirely by ship. When the Air Force discovered Metlakatla just a few miles from their base, they found it self-supporting and attractive, with gaily painted houses and streets and walks that had long ago been planked in wood. In operation was the modern salmon cannery, a hydroelectric plant which furnished power and water to the village without charge, the busy sawmill and the lovely white church.

After Alaska became a state in 1958, the residents were finally able to assume their full share of responsibility for the natives. Even now a new era is dawning for Alaska's original people.

At the invitation of the Federal Indian Bureau, tribal leaders from all the states met in Washington at a White House Conference on Indian Affairs for the purpose of creating new legislative proposals. These meetings helped the Indian Bureau shape legislative proposals into final form for the 90th Congress which convened in January, 1967.

Congress is now resolved that the new national Indian policy shall be continued "until the day when the nation's moral and legal obligations to its first citizens — the American Indians and the Alaska natives — are fulfilled."

At long last, both voices, the voices of the white man and of the Indian people, are talking on the same side of the river, and are able to hear and understand each other above the noise of the rushing water.

BIBLIOGRAPHY

Most helpful sources:

Arctander, Karl. *Apostle of Alaska.* London: Fleming Revell Co., 1909. (Lent by Florence Thornton, Woodburn, Oregon.)

British Columbia Heritage Series, *Our Native Peoples,* Tsimshian, Series 1, Volume 6. Victoria, British Columbia: Provincial Archives, Provincial Museum, 1952.

Drucker, Philip. *Indians of the Northwest Coast.* New York: American Museum of Natural History, 1963.

Inverarity, Robert Bruce. *Art of the Northwest Coast Indians.* Berkeley, California: University of California Press, 1950.

Wellcome, Sir Henry. *The Story of Metlakatla.* London: Saxon & Co., 1887.

Other reading:

Bancroft, Hubert Howe. *History of Alaska.* San Francisco: Bancroft & Co., 1886.

Bancroft, Hubert Howe. *History of British Columbia.* San Francisco: The History Company, 1890.

Boas, Franz. *Primitive Art.* New York: Dover Publications, 1955.

Carrighar, Sally. *Moonlight at Midday.* New York: Alfred Knopf, 1958.

Dockstader, Frederick J. *Indian Art in America.* Greenwich, Conn.: New York Graphic Society, 1960.

Garfield, Viola E. and Linn A. Forrest. *The Wolf and the Raven.* Seattle: University of Washington Press, 1948.

Gabrielson, Ira and Frederick Lincoln. *The Birds of Alaska.* Washington, D.C.: Wildlife Management Institute, 1957.

Gruening, Ernest H. *The State of Alaska.* New York: Random House, 1954.

Lafarge, Oliver. *A Pictorial History of the American Indian.* New York: Crown Publishers, 1956.

McInnis, Edgar. *Canada: A Political and Social History.* New York: Holt, Rinehart and Winston, Revised Edition, 1961.

Muir, John. *Travels in Alaska.* Boston: Houghton Mifflin Co., 1915.

Peck, Anne Merriman. *The Pageant of Canadian History.* New York: Longmans, Green and Co. Inc., 1943.

Pamphlet: "A Short Story of the Metlakatla Christian Mission." Copyright 1954 by the Co-Trustees of the William Duncan Trust, National Press, Palo Alto, California.

Pamphlet: "The Story of Metlakatla," by Mrs. Frederick C. Schmidt, Metlakatla Christian Mission, published between 1938 and 1944.

Canadian Hydrographic Service, Dept. of Mines and Technical Surveys, Ottawa. Charts No. 3982 and 3837.

U. S. Dept. of Commerce, Coast and Geodetic Survey, Washington Science Center, Rockville, Maryland. Chart No. 8100, year 1891; Chart No. 8075, year 1897.

U. S. Congress, 90th Congress, 1st Session, February 17, 1967. S. Concurrent Resolution 11. National American Indian and Alaska Natives policy resolution.

U. S. Board of Indian Commissioners, 18th Annual Report, Washington, D.C., 1887. Conference of Missionary Boards and Indian Rights Associations, Annual Meeting, Washington, D.C., January 6, 1887.

U. S. Dept. Interior, Office Indian Affairs, Metlakatla, Alaska. Rules and Regulations for Annette Island Reserve, Alaska, 1915.

The quotation on page 54 is from *Indians of the Northwest Coast* by Philip Drucker. Chief Toy-a-atte's speech on pages 140–143 is from *The Story of Metlakatla* by Sir Henry Wellcome, and originally appeared in *Our New Alaska* by Charles Hallock, New York: 1886.